DIRTY TEACHING

A Beginner's Guide to Learning Outdoors

JULIET ROBERTSON

independent
thinking press

First published by

Independent Thinking Press
Crown Buildings, Bancyfelin, Carmarthen, Wales, SA33 5ND, UK

and

Independent Thinking Press, PO Box 2223, Williston, VT 05495, USA

www.independentthinkingpress.com

Independent Thinking Press is an imprint of Crown House Publishing Ltd.

First published 2014. Reprinted 2014, 2015, 2017, 2018, 2019, 2020 (twice), 2021.

British Library Cataloguing-in-Publication Data.

A catalogue entry for this book is available from the British Library.

Print ISBN 978-1-78135-107-9
Mobi ISBN 978-1-78135-148-2
ePub ISBN 978-1-78135-149-9
ePDF ISBN 978-1-78135-150-5

Printed and bound in the USA by
Versa Press, East Peoria, IL

Contents

Preface

You could have heard a pine needle drop in the wood. Thirty children sat silently, scattered among the trees. Some were lost in thought. Others were scribbling notes on scrap paper. It was hard to believe that this was taking place on a still January day, five degrees below zero.

Sheltered by the young trees, we gathered to share our work. In turn we read out our chosen lines. Together we created a group poem, where every child's contribution was welcomed and valued. There was a magical, spine-tingling feel to the whole experience that was felt by all.

It did not start out this way. When I saw the children come out of the school building, I knew immediately it was *one of those classes*. The sort that challenge, question and push a teacher to the limit.

After a quick warm-up listening activity, we moved through the forest which had been planted around the perimeter of the playing field a decade earlier. The children were still tuning in to being outside. They rushed along the path, ignoring the task given to them. Some of the boys were pushing and shoving each other. This was not intentional bad behaviour. They were just excited.

So that's how we came to be writing poetry and listening to the sounds of silence. In the woodland, each child found a place where they could sit far enough away from the others. They had time to let those thoughts and feelings surface. Calm descended. The special nature of the outdoors had finally captured this class.

Acknowledgements

I believe it takes a whole community to help
an author write a book. My gratitude and thanks go
to everyone who has given support and
advice along the way.

In particular: Ian Gilbert and Independent
Thinking Limited, Caroline Lenton, the Crown
House Publishing team, my infinitely patient family,
Simon Beames, Karen Boyd, education consultant
David Cameron, Kate Coutts, Alison Drever, Judy
Duncan, Joyce Gilbert, Tim Gill, Roger Greenaway,
Fiona Hamilton, Terri Harrison, Jenny Harvey,
Jane Hewitt, Katie Iwaniw, Ursula Jardine, Adrian
King, Lynda Leyland, Magnus and Siw Linde,
Joanna Liversidge, Hywel Roberts, Sandra Lyons,
Claire Marsden, Mel McCree, Lynda Mills, Cath
Prisk, Linda and Ryan Reed, Hamish Ross, Eleanor
Sheppard, David Sobel, Dr Walter M. Stephen and
the Sir Patrick Geddes Memorial Trust,
Mark and Sarah Whelan.

Many thanks go to the following schools whose
grounds and children are featured in this book:
Athersley South Primary School, Crimond School,
Hoyland Common Primary School, Inverallochy
School, Mile End School and Pathways
Primary Academy.

Introduction

This book is for primary teachers and student teachers who want to teach outside. It is aimed at those working with six- to twelve-year-olds. The ideas are based upon my own experiences of working with classes where this is a new and different way of learning.

The majority of activities and suggestions are simple and involve minimal planning and resources. They are doable by a teacher with their class in the school grounds or local area.

Whilst training, courses and conversations with outdoor experts make a positive difference, there is no substitute for experience and knowing the children in your class. As a consequence, this book is written in the belief that teachers:

- Have the skills and competences to teach outside as well as inside. Any approach to learning and teaching usually works just as effectively outdoors as it does inside.

- Have an ability to take an idea and tweak it to make it suit the needs of the children in their class. All the ideas in this book can be refined and improved – it is a springboard for experimenting.

- Have to make an effort to learn how to teach outside on a frequent and regular basis. We have been conditioned to think 'indoors'. This is a habit that can be changed. The pay-off is very liberating and many teachers who make this change find their practice has a new lease of life.

- Have only just begun to truly appreciate the potential for learning outside and the benefits this brings in the short and long term to the well-being of children and our society, especially when the learning happens in nature.

This is not to ignore the contributions made by the vast array of professionals, organisations, volunteers, expedition organisers and residential centres to the learning which happens outside during a child's school life. However, I want to empower primary teachers to play an active part in this process too.

What is covered in this book?

There is a huge diversity of books about learning indoors. Likewise, it is impossible to do justice to the potential of learning outdoors in one book. So, this book mainly concentrates on:

■ Kick-starting the process of working outside with a class.

■ Simple outdoor ideas that a primary teacher can lead with their class of thirty pupils in the school grounds or within walking distance off-site.

■ Practical issues which arise when learning takes place outside.

The structure of the book is designed so that you can read it from cover to cover, or you can dip in and out of it as time and interest permits. I deliberately did not go down the route of detailed lessons or series of lessons. I would like the ideas and activities to be seeds of suggestion rather than directed activities.

What is outdoor learning?

Before stepping outside with a class, it can be useful to think about what outdoor learning is and why it matters. In a nutshell, outdoor learning is an umbrella term which covers every type of learning experience which happens outdoors. This could be adventurous activities, environmental education, team challenges, an international expedition or a playground game.

The beauty of this definition is that it covers little and large experiences of any sort that happen outside. What matters, however, is that – regardless of where the learning takes place – the quality of the experience is the best it can be and is authentic, meaningful and relevant for the children involved.

Ideally, we want to make the most of the unique and special nature of being outdoors. We need the variety provided by:

■ The weather – imagine a world without rainbows: the sunshine and the rain are key ingredients.

■ The seasons – these bring variety throughout the year, adding interest to our lives and festivals that celebrate the cyclical events.

■ The space and freedom of the world beyond the classroom.

■ The landscape – whether this is urban, wild or somewhere in-between.

Many teachers assume that outdoor learning is a subject, discipline or curriculum area. Some consider outdoor learning as an approach to learning, as just one of many tools in a teacher's toolbox. For me, it is about making the most of any place or space outside of the traditional school walls.

It's about relationships

It can be helpful to think of the learning that happens as a result of the relationships between people, the nature of the activity and the place and time where it takes place.

The idea of using *place* as a key part of the learning process comes from the work of Sir Patrick Geddes (1854–1932), a Scottish town planner, biologist and educator, known for his progressive views, who developed the concept of 'think global, act local'. He also advocated a 'hands, heart, head' approach to learning.[1]

Most initiatives and ideas within education focus on activities and people. For example, reams of advice is available on improving literacy. Yet, this is largely focused upon motivating children and activities which encourage and support children to develop confidence in this area.

Where children read and how this impacts on the acquisition of literacy skills tends to be ignored. It also means that a huge range of possibilities is being missed when you think of the choice of locations in which we could learn. Think of all the places where people freely read, such as a novel on the beach or a newspaper on the bus. It rarely happens at a table with a group of people of a similar age taking turns to read a paragraph aloud, other than in a school.

Time matters too. During the course of a day, the weather and light changes, impacting upon any outdoor place. The seasons bring annual variety and so do the years. If you think about how a three-year-old child might walk down a street, their behaviour and perspective is very different to that of a teenager.

To forget about the impact of place is like removing one leg from a three-legged stool. The stool is permanently out of balance and much harder to sit on. Ignoring the influence of place when teaching makes your job a lot harder. Nature has inspired generations of artists, writers, inventors and scientists to create and innovate. Thus, as teachers, we can use different places and spaces innovatively to inspire our children.

i Have a cuppa

Have a break. Make yourself a hot drink and take it outside. Drink it there instead of where you usually sit inside and compare the experience.

■   What are the similarities and what are the differences?

---

1   P. Higgins and R. Nicol, Professor Sir Patrick Geddes: 'Vivendo Discimus' – By Living We Learn. In C. Knapp and T. Smith (eds), *Sourcebook for Experiential Education: Key Thinkers and their Contributions* (New York: Routledge, 2011) pp. 32–40.

■ What did you notice about your thoughts and behaviour (e.g. where you sat and how, or did you stand the entire time)?

■ What would you change or do differently if you took your cup of tea outside again?

This activity should show you that often people think and behave differently in different places. It is likely that you do not have a comfy sofa outside, so you may have chosen to wander around the garden with your cup of tea. You may have felt quite cold. Perhaps you were keeping a sharp eye on a nearby gull in case it tried to steal your Jaffa Cake!

What this means is that you need to be prepared for children behaving differently outside, especially if they have not spent much time undertaking formal lessons outdoors. Everyone will need time to acclimatise.

What places outside?

Learning can happen in any outdoor space. For convenience, using the school grounds makes a lot of sense as less time, preparation and money are involved. The supervision ratios tend to be the same as for inside, which means you can take your class outside without needing to rely on volunteers or other staff to support you.

Many schools and nurseries have a designated place off-site, such as a wood, which is used on a frequent and regular basis for a variety of activities. Whilst this can take a bit of time and effort to establish both the site and the routines around its use, the effort is worth it. Often it is a very good way of establishing positive community links with different organisations and professionals.

ii Your life in places

> How hard it is to escape from places. However carefully one goes they hold you – you leave little bits of yourself fluttering on the fences – like rags and shreds of your very life.
> Katherine Mansfield

Think back across your life. Write down your thoughts in response to the questions below. It is useful if you can discuss these with other people, especially the final question.

■ Which places are most important to you and why?

■ When you are on holiday, what do you miss most of all?

■ What is it about the community, culture and landscape of where you live that you most strongly identify with?

■ How can you apply this to your teaching?

Make learning sticky

If you consider your own time at school, the chances are that your strongest memories will be about your time outdoors. This will include residential stays, excursions and playtimes. For some reason, we appear to remember more outdoor activities even though it is quite likely we spent less time outside than in.

Such memories are important for two reasons. Firstly, there is an onus on us to provide lessons in an environment that is conducive to learning, both in the long and short term. Common sense suggests that if being outside is more memorable, then this may be one way of helping children to remember what they have learned. Secondly, we need to consider why the memories stick. What is it about being outside that contributes to making an event memorable?

Chip and Dan Heath spent over ten years looking at why some ideas take hold and others are forgotten. In their book, *Made to Stick*, they suggest that there are six principles which make a story, headline or other experience impact on our memory.[2] These are neatly summed up as the SUCCES formula: Simple, Unexpected, Concrete, Credible, Emotional, Stories.

An event or experience does not need to contain all of the principles which can be applied to any learning, outside or inside. However, they easily lend themselves to the outdoors. It is naturally 'sticky'. For example:

- **Simple:** Less is often more. Most activities outside rely on materials found *in situ* and the imagination of those involved.

- **Unexpected:** Outdoor activities often end up being interrupted. A cat might walk through the playground. A patch of mushrooms may be discovered behind a bush. View these interruptions as a vital part of the lesson and go with the flow; even if your original learning objective is not met, another one can easily replace it.

- **Concrete:** Outdoor experiences tend to link better to actual events, people and the community. Often practical skills are required. This makes the learning authentic and real.

- **Credible:** Working outside seems to naturally lend itself to children's lives and interests. The outdoors is multisensory so children acquire an understanding through using lots of their senses.

- **Emotional:** This is the 'ooh', 'ah', 'ugh' factor. Not all time spent outside is pleasant but when you hear these sorts of sounds coming from your class, you know that a connection is being made. Learning is an emotional process as much as a cognitive one.

- **Stories:** It is relatively easy to create a narrative of outdoor experiences. It is much harder to do this when sitting down and completing a page of work in an exercise book. We can use stories as a springboard to an outdoor activity – we can make up stories and act them out. Adventures are often recalled as narratives.

---

2 C. Heath and D. Heath, *Made to Stick: Why Some Ideas Take Hold and Others Come Unstuck* (London: Random House, 2007).

Being mindful of these principles when planning outdoor experiences may help to make the learning memorable.

iii Look for SUCCES in your lessons

Ask children in your class to recall a lesson or activity from a few months ago. What made that experience so memorable? See if you can link what the children say to the SUCCES formula (see page 5). It is also worth trying this in terms of lessons or events that stick out in your mind from your own school days.

Why does learning outside matter?

Many adults who work with young people can give personal accounts of the enjoyment, freedom, creativity and inspiration that outdoor experiences offer children. The benefits of learning outside have been recognised and documented at least as far back as the fourteenth century.[3]

---

3 R. Joyce, *Outdoor Learning Past and Present* (Maidenhead: Open University Press, 2012), pp. 11–21.

In the past two or three decades, a substantial amount of research has been undertaken which all points in the direction of humans needing nature not just to survive but to thrive.[4] Our cognitive, social, emotional and physical health is affected by time spent outside, especially when in a natural space. This is why there is a growing emphasis on using green spaces, such as beaches and woodlands, in education. It is also why naturalising school grounds to increase plant cover and encourage wildlife makes a positive contribution to children's well-being.

The literature and research in this area suggest that outdoor learning, as part of a planned approach, may:

■ Increase attainment in specific subjects.

■ Impact positively on the health and well-being of young people.

■ Help develop responsible citizens and lifelong appreciation of the natural world.

■ Improve the social and communication skills of young people.

■ Effectively weave together many of the strands of education for sustainable development.[5]

The parallels between all of the approaches to learning outdoors include:

■ Interdisciplinary learning across subject areas.

■ The use of the school grounds and local neighbourhoods, especially greenspace.

■ Continuous visits over a long period of time, rather than one-off trips.

■ Children involved in the planning and decision-making.

■ Routines that develop skills and build independence.

■ Teaching and learning in, through and about the natural and man-made world.

If you want to find out more about research and robust arguments for outdoor learning, then read *Learning Outside the Classroom* by Simon Beames, Robbie Nicol and Pete Higgins.[6] It provides a very accessible summary with lots of practical advice aimed at primary and middle school teachers.

---

4 Visit <http://creativestarlearning.co.uk/support/outdoor-learning-research/> for links to some of the main outdoor learning research websites.

5 Visit <http://www.unesco.org.uk/education_for_sustainable_development> to find out more about the United Nations Decade of Education for Sustainable Development.

6 S. Beames, R. Nicol and P. Higgins, *Learning Outside the Classroom: Theory and Guidelines for Practice* (New York: Routledge, 2011).

CHAPTER 1

The Golden Principles of Teaching Outdoors

As teachers, we have beliefs and values that determine how we teach. They shape what we say and do. When working outside over the past few years, I have found it helpful to:

- Take a sustainable and rights-based approach.

- Value free play and playful learning.

- Provide a nurturing, natural environment.

- Develop children's creative capacities.

For me, these are golden principles because they stand the test of time and change in education. I use them to ensure that I think about the wider purpose of learning outdoors and its contribution to providing children with the best possible education. It is an essential part of making a difference to every child I teach.

Whilst the future may be uncertain, with uncertainty comes opportunity, especially in a rapidly changing society. Therefore, I believe it is our responsibility to help children develop a growth mindset and acquire the practical skills, compassion and empathy in order to live harmoniously and help one another.

A sustainable and rights-based approach

> The best time to plant a tree was twenty years ago. The next best time is now.
>
> Chinese proverb

We need to consider the environmental impact of any outdoor lesson, as we do with any other aspect of our teaching. Over the years, we should be making our school grounds and local spaces into better places as a result of our stewardship. If we have a right to use a place, we have a responsibility to care for it.

My belief is that children need outdoor experiences to understand big issues such as climate change. This includes opportunities to experience wild or semi-wild spaces. As they get older, getting involved in collaborative, action-based projects in the local community may also be relevant. It demonstrates that we can all play our part in looking after ourselves, our communities and our local places and wildlife. Families should be included so that children see close agreement between school and home about the importance of sustainability, and participate in discussions and action in both places. Very often, children will initiate this if they are part of the ethos and approach at school.

We know children need the space and time to play freely outside in nature. Yet, it needs to go hand in hand with a developmentally appropriate progression of wider experiences that encourage children to care for nature and to have a basic understanding of natural processes. This was picked up by Nicol et al. when reviewing outdoor learning research:

> Simply 'being outdoors' is not sufficient for young people to express an ethic of care for nature or develop an understanding of natural processes. These things seem to be learned when they are an explicit aim of experiential activities and when they are mediated in appropriate ways.[1]

Adults need to model appropriate behaviour and attitudes too. Sustainable development education is a much deeper matter than remembering to pick up litter or save energy. Make sure you know what sustainability means and how you can incorporate your country's guidelines for sustainable development education into your class routines and practice.

The rights-based approach is two-fold. Firstly, it creates a more child-centred, reflective and positive framework for considering how to teach the big concepts and ideas behind sustainability. It dovetails neatly into the Rights Respecting Schools Award[2] and recognises that the UN Convention on the Rights of a Child[3] needs to underpin educational practice.

Secondly, most countries have laws about what the public can or cannot do when out in the countryside. It is all too often forgotten that responsibilities go hand-in-hand with rights. For example, in Scotland there is a public right to beachcomb on the foreshore. This is the tidal section between the high-water mark at the top of the beach and the water line. However, with this right comes various responsibilities, such as:

- ■ Being able to identify your finds so that you know what you are taking and can make a sensible decision as to whether it is okay to pick it up or not.

- ■ Gathering finds sustainably and only removing a very small sample, or just taking photos.

---

1 R., Nicol, P. Higgins, H. Ross and G. Mannion, *Outdoor Education in Scotland: A Summary of Recent Research*. (Perth and Glasgow: Scottish Natural Heritage, 2007). Available at: <http://www.snh.gov.uk/publications-data-and-research/publications/search-the-catalogue/publication-detail/?id=852>, p. 5.

2 See <http://www.unicef.org.uk/Get-Involved/Your-organisation/Schools/rights-respecting-school-award/>

3 Unicef, Fact Sheet: A Summary of the Rights under the Convention on the Rights of the Child. Available at: <http://www.unicef.org/crc/files/Rights_overview.pdf>

- Knowing and understanding the tidal system on a particular beach.

- Behaving in a manner that does not disturb other users or wildlife.

In this example, a sustainable and rights-based emphasis shifts the health and safety concerns about tides and good practice when working near water into a more positive context of knowing and respecting the environment.

Idea 1.1 Know your rights

Find out about the laws in your country relating to access rights. Have a think about how these can be used to develop children's understanding of how to care for the countryside and as a positive framework for outdoor activities. Think about:

- What behaviours will need to be modelled by adults?

- Are there any games, stories or activities that can be used to reinforce key points or issues? I find these approaches more effective than simply a discussion before going outside.

- What routines can be set up which would help to embed a sustainable and rights-based approach?

Value free play and take a playful approach to learning

> If you want creative workers, give them enough time to play.
>
> John Cleese

We have a paradox in schools. We accept the value of play, especially in the Early Years, but the idea of play in the primary sector and beyond often does not feel like a legitimate use of the precious time available.

For some children, school playtimes may be the only informal outdoor play opportunities available to them on a regular basis. It is a time for children to recharge their batteries between lessons. Some children find their lives are full of structured activities, such as music lessons and sports classes, or spend lots of time doing sedentary activities, such as playing computer games. Others may live in places where going out to play is not possible.

As part of developing learning outdoors, you can demonstrate that you value playtimes and facilitate daily outdoor free-play opportunities, regardless of the weather, season and the ability of a child to play with others or complete their work.

11

There are many different types of play. However, it is 'free play' which we need to encourage during breaktimes. Play is often described by play experts as happening when children choose what they want to do and how they want to do it. It is child-initiated and child-led with no external goals or rewards.[4] This is how children learn to socialise, develop independence, improve their physical coordination and enjoy themselves without adults directing proceedings. It is how they learn about grit and resilience, power and control, to apologise and make friends.

A lot happens at breaktimes. As educators, we can look for opportunities to capitalise upon this and to acknowledge the contribution of playtimes to the rest of children's time in school. Children appreciate creative, as well as physical, play opportunities – particularly in nature-rich outdoor spaces. I often hear teachers and children comment positively about such experiences and how it helps children to be more settled and better able to concentrate when back in class. The health benefits associated with free play are numerous and include increased physical activity, improved physical and mental health, well-being, and social and emotional development.[5]

---

4 This is an abbreviated version of the definition given in J. Santer and C. Griffiths, with D. Goodall, *Free Play in Early Childhood: A Literature Review* (London: Play England and the National Children's Bureau, 2007). Available at: <http://www.playengland.org.uk/media/120426/free-play-in-early-childhood.pdf>, p. xi.

5 J. Gleave and I. Cole-Hamilton, *A World without Play: A Literature Review* (London: Play England, 2012). Available at: <http://www.playengland.org.uk/media/371031/a-world-without-play-literature-review-2012.pdf>, p. 3.

If your school keeps children inside during inclement weather, you will know how this affects the class time afterwards – cabin fever! The primary schools who enable children to play outdoors all year round and in all weathers, find the benefits outweigh the hassles of managing wet clothes and mud.

As a teacher, you may feel you do not have much say in whole-school approaches to play. However, the children in your class will have plenty of opinions about the subject and may consider this a worthwhile matter to take forward to their pupil council or other child-led committees.

When it comes to thinking about play in the context of learning outdoors, we need to bear in mind the following factors:

- The informal learning that happens during breaks, lunchtimes and out of school – think about how much of the curriculum may be being covered during this time.

- The need for children to have daily free play experiences and to simply be able to play for the sake of it.

- The inclusion of play as a valid part of formal learning which happens during class time – this may be more directed than at playtimes so is not necessarily free play.

- The use of playtime activity as a stimulus to formal work during class times.

- Naturalising and making the school grounds play-friendly spaces (this is considered in Chapter 9).

- Different types of play can be facilitated by the right social and physical environments (e.g. social, role play, team games, journeying).

A playful approach to learning is very different to free play. A playful approach tends to be planned for by a teacher and is usually adult-initiated and adult-led. Generally there are specific learning outcomes in mind.

However there is a place for this during class time. A playful approach makes learning fun. Being asked to gather round and look at a wildflower and listen to the teacher talk about the functions of different parts of a plant is dull. Instead, it is better for children to make a personal connection to a plant in some way. For example, after undertaking a weeding activity, set aside time for children to play with the leaves, stems and roots they have removed. Ask them what they want to do next, in terms of finding out more about a plant's structure and its functions. You may be surprised how much they will strive to teach themselves when given an incentive, a supportive environment and not much structure.

A playful approach also brings variety. It is easy to develop confidence in one type of outdoor activity and stick to this. Yet, we all know variety is the spice of life, so planning and undertaking a range of playful outdoor activities helps.

Provide a nurturing, natural environment

> I never teach my pupils; I only attempt to provide the conditions in which they can learn.
>
> Albert Einstein

A nurturing, natural environment is my description for an outdoor space which truly meets the needs of the children who play there. It is about providing a place that benefits their health and well-being. It sends a strong message that children are welcome and valued.

As a result of a two-year research project, *Special Places; Special People*, Wendy Titman demonstrated that school grounds, by design, influence the way children behave. She suggested that children seek a range of opportunities from an environment which is 'required to offer the potential for children to "do" and "think" and "feel" and "be" all at the same time'.[6]

Greenspaces, especially areas that feel wild, appear to have a particularly positive effect. They are calmer environments – places to think, be and experience time out from the stresses and strains of everyday life. The constant rhythms of the natural world, such as day and night, the seasons and

---

6 W. Titman, *Special Places; Special People: The Hidden Curriculum of School Grounds* (Winchester: World Wide Fund for Nature/ Learning through Landscapes, 1993), p. 58.

the weather, provide consistency for children, especially those who live chaotic lives.

Children will actively seek out different ways of interacting with features in the landscape. Woods, beaches and other natural spaces offer great potential in terms of how they can be utilised for play and learning. By contrast, asphalt playgrounds with fixed equipment rarely offer the range of play opportunities children need to explore and challenge themselves.

Finally, we need to consider the activities we offer children outside and how these contribute to developing resilience so they are able to look after themselves and others.

Developing children's creative capacities

By creating we think, by living we learn.

Sir Patrick Geddes

Creativity is a term that means different things to different people. It is often assumed to refer to subjects such as art, drama, dance or music, which can offer much scope to be creative. However, so do science, the social sciences, technology and many other facets of human activity.

It is the innovation, the motivation, the drive and the passion of any person, group or community wanting to change and improve circumstances that is the linchpin of creativity. If we have the capacity to imagine, innovate and ensure our efforts have value to humanity, then we have the potential to shape the future. This can give us a sense of control over our destiny and that of our pupils. We can see the impact of what we have set out to achieve and this further encourages us to be active and engaged. This is the gift of creativity.

As teachers, our job is to look at the outdoors in terms of its potential for developing creative capacities, such as:

- Positive risk-taking and management.
- Divergent as well as convergent thinking and ideas generation.
- Being able to transfer and apply skills and concepts in new and different ways.
- Finding practical solutions to everyday problems.

- Channelling our feelings and emotions to enable creative activity.

- A growth mindset and a go-for-it attitude.

- Spontaneity and improvisation.

- Being able to contemplate.

For me, the outdoors is a living, breathing example of possibility, of all that creativity is about. All ideas stem from nature, one way or the other. Most innovations mimic the natural world. We just have to look at it with fresh eyes, curiosity and an enquiring mind.

Thus, children spending time outside and getting to know the world around them through being able to experience it in different ways matters. In recent years, there has been a rise in evidence which suggests that contact with nature is highly beneficial.[7] Natural spaces appear to help us relax – they make us feel more rested and enable us to concentrate. When playing outside, children often demonstrate high levels of imagination, such as using bits of bark as plates in role play.

The use of natural materials often encourages higher-order thinking. For example, if you ask your class to make a one metre line with uniform interlocking bricks, this will produce a very specific response. If the children use stones or shells instead, then a variety of results will transpire, none of

---

7 See, for example, E. Selhub and A. Logan, *Your Brain on Nature: The Science of Nature's Influence on Your Health, Happiness and Vitality* (Toronto: HarperCollins, 2012).

which will be wrong. Very often, using natural resources gives rise to focused discussions between children and generates further challenge-based explorations, such as seeing if every group can make a one metre line with exactly the same number of stones.

Taking learning outdoors asks us to rethink our practice and question our values. We have to think on our feet and be responsive to the unpredictable world beyond our indoor classrooms. To ensure that children maintain the levels of creativity shown in the Early Years, we have to model creativity in our teaching.

Idea 1.2 Build a tower

Building a tower from different materials works well with most adults, from parent groups to education staff. It helps people to compare the use of natural and man-made materials in an educational context.

Ask pairs or small groups to create a tower using five pieces of Lego. Next, repeat the activity using stones. Afterwards, discuss what happened. You may wish to focus on the level of challenge, problem-solving, amount of social interaction and group work.

The Golden Principles of Learning Outdoors checklist

Have you:

- Found out what you need to know about education for sustainable development to ensure you embed the expectations into your outdoor work?

- Got a copy of the Countryside Code,[8] or your country's equivalent, and thought about how you can use this constructively to set expectations about learning outside?

- Considered what you believe matters to you about learning outdoors? Perhaps you would choose different principles and, if so, what would they be and why?

- Read up on any aspect of the principles which you feel you need to know more about?

---

8 See <http://www.naturalengland.org.uk/ourwork/enjoying/countrysidecode/default.aspx>

CHAPTER 2

Before You Go Outside

Building outdoor activities into your daily or weekly routine is not dissimilar to going on a diet or developing a fitness routine. It is about developing a habit. It can be a tough and painful process, leaving you feeling deflated when you have just delivered a less than perfect lesson or the children have run amok outside.

Yet it can also leave you hungry for more when a wonderful lesson happens. I once watched a four-year-old child who was totally blind complete a sensory rope trail. It was like watching a professional concert pianist at work. She used her fingers so tenderly and sensitively to explore the different objects and her surroundings, guided by the rope. This was one of the most profound moments of my life as a teacher.

It is tempting to blame external circumstances for preventing us from teaching outside. Yet, ultimately, the responsibility is on us as individuals to get over this and get out there. We have to find ways of supporting ourselves through the process so that we can take the rough with the smooth.

Catch 22: develop the habit of working outside

Many years ago, I heard that it takes twenty-two days to make or break a habit. This resonated with my experiences of changing my own practice.

Like any other change, thinking and working outside requires a certain amount of discipline and effort. There is a need for a frequent and regular approach. The more often you go outside, the easier and more normal it becomes. The ideal is to aim for a situation where being outside requires no more planning, preparation or effort than teaching indoors. This does take time, so having a target, such as twenty-two sessions, means you give yourself and the class the time needed to change the indoor habit!

I have found the easiest method has been to aim for a weekly session outside throughout the year. This is doable, even through the winter months. Also, when the summer arrives, if you have been going out through the winter, the amount of time you spend outside tends to naturally increase.

Think about other initiatives and changes that you have been asked to make as a teacher, and consider how long these have taken to embed. Some are quite quick, like remembering to walk on one side of the corridor. However, it may take a year or more to become comfortable with a new approach to teaching reading or writing.

It goes without saying that you may find it takes less time or more. It depends on many factors. I was caught out when I first began to go outside regularly. I had a lovely Year 1 class and I thought they would acclimatise quickly. However, the children had never had regular outdoor experiences, not even in nursery, so everything we did was new, different and wildly exciting for them. Sitting quietly was out of the question for several sessions. I was also surprised by the children's lack of care for the environment. I found I had to plan and prepare the class in simply knowing how to 'be' outdoors.

If you are working with very young children, you may already be going out more often. If this is the case, then make a plan about how much you wish to increase the amount of time spent outside. For example, increasing numbers of nurseries have 'Welly Wednesdays' or 'Outdoor Thursdays' where the whole session is spent outside, including being dropped off and picked up by parents.

Begin with yourself in mind

Beginning with yourself may sound extraordinarily selfish for a teacher. It is ingrained into the culture of our profession that children come first: they are the priority; we are selfless beings.

Being outside is different. It's like the airplane emergency guidance which tells you to put on your oxygen mask before sticking one on your child. *You* have to be prepared before you can support your class through the process of working outside.

So, here is the 'love yourself' guide to getting outside.

Idea 2.1 Dress comfortably

You need to feel warm and comfortable outside and bear in mind that with children you are more likely to get messy. Chalk may end up on your knees. Grass stains magically appear on your bum. Somehow the elbow on your jacket gets ripped on a hidden piece of wire. Dress as if you plan for these things to happen and remember it's probably best to leave the high-tech outdoor gear at home.

Shop around for some suitable clothes and footwear that passes muster. Wearing outdoor clothing that you love and want to use is a good incentive and makes it easier to get outside. It is also important to be well wrapped up because it can take a long time to warm up again if you get cold.

Other things to remember include:

- Layers of clothes are warmer than one big bulky item. It also means that you can adapt between indoors and outdoors more easily by adding and removing layers as necessary.

- Cotton, which includes denim, is cold when wet and takes ages to dry. This also means your underwear, so don't sit down on grass without a portable seat unless you like having a wet patch on your rear and children giggling behind you.

- Wellies can be very cold in winter, so put thermal insoles inside them and wear thick, wool socks.

- If you get cold feet then try keeping your legs warmer – wear long ski socks or welly boot socks in winter.

- If you hate wearing a hat, then donning a warm scarf and ear muffs can be a good alternative. I have been told that berets will not give you 'hat hair' but they just fall off my head!

- A pair of cheap fleece gloves is handy, especially if you are using chalk – and they avoid fingernails being accidently scuffed on the ground.

- Wear a sun hat and sunscreen on sunny days.

Some teachers find that keeping a pair of wellies and a waterproof jacket and over-trousers at school means they are always prepared for going outside.

Idea 2.2 Eat and drink plenty

It is very likely that when you are outside you will be more physically active and will burn up more calories. If it is a cold day, you will need to move around to keep yourself warm. This exercise is an effortless piece of multi-tasking which will earn you an extra biscuit at breaktime!

Remember to drink enough fluids. Dehydration is really unpleasant and can make you bad-tempered at the very least. If you think your children need a bottle of water with them outside, then you do too.

Idea 2.3 Make a plan and share the love

As the saying goes, 'If you fail to plan, then you plan to fail'. Planning is essential when starting to go outside. If you have to submit your plans to your head teacher or another member of the senior leadership team, then they can discuss these with you and offer feedback. Other useful approaches to planning include:

Sharing the plan with your class

Your class will have lots of good suggestions as to why they should be learning outside and the sorts of things they might enjoy. Put a chart up on the wall and note the date, activity and pupil rating. Shared evaluations of outdoor sessions can help to build a collaborative learning environment inside and out. It makes a good focus for a class blog too.

Having a 'think outdoors' wall

Children can add their ideas, tips and suggestions to an interactive 'think outdoors' space. You could include routines and advice as well as activities on the wall. Ask the children to find ideas and activities on the Internet. Encourage them to think about different games and activities they play during lunchtime and breaks. How could these be adapted to a formal learning situation?

Working with a supportive colleague

Talk about your outdoor sessions with colleagues and ask them for tips, ideas and advice. If another teacher is also trying to get outside more, it can be fun to do a couple of shared sessions where both classes spend time together outdoors.

If you have a planning, preparation and assessment slot during the school day, agree to support each other at the beginning. It can be reassuring to have a friend or colleague to work alongside your class and vice versa. Team teaching can provide a powerful way to learn from each other too.

Idea 2.4 Play to your strengths and those of your children

We all have strengths and weaknesses as teachers. If there is a particular subject or curriculum area that you feel more confident teaching, then stick with this when you first venture outside. Start with what you can do well and what you're comfortable with. This will give you a greater chance of success and job satisfaction.

You also need to consider the strengths of your class. A group that likes technology work inside will probably enjoy technology projects outside too.

Idea 2.5 Keep it simple

Aim for a series of simple grab 'n' go activities (such as those outlined in Chapter 3). You need to make getting outside a success for you and your class. In the beginning, you will be doing a lot of planning and organising in terms of setting up routines around working outside, so the actual activities need to be straightforward.

Idea 2.6 Expect the worst and hope for the best

Feeling nervous can sometimes be an asset. It means you are more likely to meticulously plan your outdoor activities, make them realistic and achievable, and keep a good eye on the children's well-being and engagement. Make the most of your fears and worries as part of your planning and preparation – this is a positive use of the energy spent worrying. Have a look at Chapter 11, which considers some of the common concerns when starting out.

Additional matters to consider include:

- Establish rules around going to the toilet. Remember that children usually go in and out of the school at breaktime to access toilets, so probably will not require an adult escort during class times. Remind children to go before going outside.

- Make sure everyone knows what to do if the fire alarm sounds. Some schools expect teachers to take a register outside with them.

- Know how to get help should you need it. You may use the same system as you do indoors. You may also be able to use a walkie-talkie or simply have the school phone number on a mobile phone.

- Read up on school policies about working outside. If you are taking a class off-site then additional procedures will need to be followed. If your school does not have guidelines then find out what advice is available from the local authority and/or national government. Do not undertake an activity which has been classed as 'adventurous' without an appropriate qualification. If in doubt, ask!

- Double check the specific needs and concerns of individual children. Put in place a plan to manage any specific issues around supporting a child to participate successfully in outdoor activities. If a child has an individual education plan or risk assessment, then incorporate the aims, approaches and strategies into this.

- Remember to brief any supporting adults about their role and remit. Check they are able to carry out the required duties.

Idea 2.7 Activities involving remote supervision

With some outdoor activities, especially ones that involve orienteering or trail-type hikes, children will be out of sight of an adult for some of the time. Therefore, you and the children need to have agreed procedures about remote supervision. These may already be part of your school or local authority policy and may include:

- Regular check-ins at agreed times.

- Informing the class teacher if going to the toilet.

- How to seek help if someone gets hurt.

- What to do if an unexpected visitor appears, including stray dogs.

- What to do if they get lost (e.g. hug a tree, call out, wait).

- That children are deemed responsible or capable enough to be supervised remotely.

Know your patch

Very few class teachers walk into a class on the first day of term at 9 a.m. without having spent some time beforehand organising the layout and putting resources in the right place. Taking your class outside without having explored the school grounds and local area is no different – preparation and planning are essential.

However, it should not be an onerous process. Below are some factors you should consider.

Idea 2.8 Finding out how you get outside

Whilst many schools have direct access from the classroom to the school grounds, some involve an exit plan akin to escaping from Alcatraz, with alarms going off the moment you touch the door handle! Some doors are locked, others don't shut properly once they are opened and occasionally there are plain nasty ones which attempt to slam shut before you've put a foot outside.

Idea 2.9 Walking the school boundary

By walking the boundary, you can see just how much space you have and where the formal and informal exit and entrance routes are. Any child who is serious about running off will know all the 'rabbit holes' in a fence. This can also help you understand when visitors suddenly appear from nowhere (in one school where I worked, many parents would jump into the school grounds via a corner wall).

Look for areas which would work well for different activities. For example:

- Where are good gathering places for your children?

- Which spots are nice and sheltered?

- Where is the best place for noisy activities which will not disturb other children working inside?

You must report any health and safety concerns you see and cannot deal with in passing – this is part of every educator's duties. For example, if you see a big branch hanging off a tree and think it might break, then find out who needs to know so that it can be checked out. If you are in doubt, then follow your school's health and safety reporting procedures.

The Royal Society for the Prevention of Accidents (RoSPA) promotes the idea of making places and situations 'as safe as necessary, not as safe as possible', which can be helpful in terms of taking a sensible approach to health and safety, inside and out.[1]

Idea 2.10 Explore your local area

By walking around your local area, you will discover its hidden gems. The better you know the area, the more easily you can use it for projects and activities. I know of one nursery class that discovered a beautiful wood tucked away behind a fly-tipping site. Since being used for a Forest Kindergarten, the mess has been cleared up and a community action group, established by parent volunteers, now looks after the woodland.

Idea 2.11 Create a risk–benefit assessment for the use of your outdoor space during class time

As its name suggests, a risk–benefit assessment is an approach to risk management which considers the benefits of any activity alongside the risks. It is a concept which is supported by the Health and Safety Executive in their high-level statement, 'Children's Play and Leisure: Promoting a Balanced Approach'.[2] It is about taking a balanced and proportionate approach to the risk-assessment process. There is a growing awareness that children want and need challenging experiences which involve a degree of risk. Applying workplace risk-management systems to schools will not meet the needs of children without appropriate modification. The National Children's Bureau's *Managing Risk in Play Provision Implementation Guide* provides the context, legal framework and practical information about risk–benefit assessments and is a must-read for all educators.[3]

You may have standard risk assessment forms which must be used. In this situation, I add an extra box or page which notes the benefits of the activity. I find this to be a helpful part of the planning process. Thinking through the benefits can enable an activity to happen for all the right reasons. It also allows me to reframe any risks as a valuable part of the outdoor learning experience for all children. For example, I may perceive a muddy patch of ground to be a 'slips and trips' risk.

---

1 For more information on safety in schools visit the RoSPA website: <http://www.rospa.com>

2 See Health and Safety Executive, Children's Play and Leisure: Promoting a Balanced Approach (n.d.). Available at <http://www.hse.gov.uk/entertainment/childs-play-statement.htm>

3 D. Ball, T. Gill and B. Spiegal, *Managing Risk in Play Provision: Implementation Guide* (London: National Children's Bureau, 2013). Available at: <http://www.playengland.org.uk/media/172644/managing-risk-in-play-provision.pdf>

However, muddy areas are hugely popular places to play! The children also develop physical coordination skills by walking through mud. Learning how to negotiate this sort of ground can better prepare them for dealing with ice and other slippery conditions.

I enjoy seeing how children's confidence and independence grow as they learn to deal with the challenges of learning outside. For example, I have often witnessed children who struggle to behave well in class, persist with lighting a fire and being vigilant about following agreed safety procedures without reminders.

Another useful and succinct document to read is *Nothing Ventured: Balancing Benefits and Risks in the Outdoors* by Tim Gill, a writer and researcher whose work focuses on childhood and risk.[4] It contains lots of facts and snippets of information. It is also affirming about the skills and capacities of teachers to make informed professional judgements to support responsible approaches to risk-taking.

Idea 2.12 Involve children in the risk–benefit assessment process

Children naturally risk assess when they play. For example, if a child doesn't feel able to climb up a tree all the way to the top, they will tend to stop where they feel most comfortable. Thus, common sense suggests that we need to separate those risks which can be self-assessed by a child from those that require a specific teaching input.

When formally involving children in the process of risk assessment, ensure this happens in a developmentally appropriate way which makes sense to the children. For example:

- Focus on what children can do.

- Explore the benefits of the activity and why it is happening.

- Explain the need for any particular safety measures that are in place.

- Allow opportunities for children to ask questions, explore their feelings, offer suggestions and have their say. A very child-centred approach is taken in the primary school series of books 'Health for Life'.[5] The strategies and activities can be easily adapted for a range of outdoor activities.

- Use stories and games which assist children to learn strategies for managing a range of circumstances and situations. For example, to help young children learn what to do if they find themselves lost, they can play a game of tag where they are safe from being caught if they hug a tree. Next, they work in pairs to meet a tree, where one child is blindfolded and has to

---

4 T. Gill, *Nothing Ventured: Balancing Benefits and Risks in the Outdoors*. Nottingham: English Outdoor Council. Available at: <http://www.englishoutdoorcouncil.org/wp-content/uploads/Nothing-Ventured.pdf>

5 See <http://www.health-for-life.org.uk>

feel the tree to get to know it. When the blindfold is removed, the child has to find their tree again. After a review, the children learn that if they are lost they should stay where they are and hug a tree.

Idea 2.13 Take a positive approach to risk

Adults need to model appropriate risk-taking. This means being genuinely up for stretching yourself in your own teaching and accepting that this may sometimes involve an activity not going to plan, or not even knowing the outcome. This is important to emphasise in a collaborative learning environment.

We also need to be mindful about our interactions with children and reflective about the level of autonomy they have to develop the skills and awareness needed to manage practical aspects of their lives. For instance:

- Do we facilitate and encourage children to take a variety of risks and be up for challenges?

- What about our own body language? Do we act in ways which clearly show we trust children to manage well in a variety of situations?

- Think about the language we use and the activities we give children around assessing risk. Are we inadvertently telling the children how dangerous life is out there? Or are we encouraging a sense of adventure and exploration of the big wide world?

- Are we aware and responsive to the children in our class? This is where dynamic risk assessment occurs. We should use our professional judgement and common sense to decide the level of intervention necessary at any given moment in time.

Resources needed for going outside

There are three key messages about resourcing for outdoor activities:

1   The environment, built or natural, is the main resource and inspiration.

2   You, the teacher, and your children are the other main resource.

3   Anything else is a bonus.

This is a useful starting point in that, if your school is short on funds, you can still go outside and teach. It also means that any special resources you have access to simply extend the possibilities rather than detract from the outdoor experience.

I appreciate that advocating a resource-free approach to teaching outdoors is a little extreme, so I collect all sorts of materials as teaching aids outside. Generally, I try to use ex-household items and old or unwanted indoor teaching resources. If they get lost or worn out, it matters less and means they are more likely to be easily replaceable. It is also a good message to children: that everything doesn't need to be nice and new, and that specific resources are not necessarily required for specific activities. It is also part of a sustainable approach to learning outdoors.

If you need to take equipment outside:

- Think about what you need to do your job.

- Encourage each child to take their own items (e.g. pencil, clipboard, seat, jacket).

- Take spares of everything, including batteries for cameras.

- Know where everything is going to be put outside (e.g. against a wall, hung on a fence, carried in a bag by each group).

- Have a place for equipment to go back to indoors.

- Make sure wet gear is dried before storing – otherwise, it may end up getting really smelly with fungal life forms of mysterious sorts using it as a habitat!

Idea 2.14 Put together a basic set of resources

I try to keep resources to a minimum. The following is a list of those I tend to use most frequently:

Pencils

Pencils work outside whether it's wet or dry. Always take along a few extra as they get misplaced or broken. Don't bother with erasers.

Scrap paper and card

Mini notebooks made from A4 paper cut into quarters and stapled together are handy. Small booklets or thin card flap around less than big sheets of A4 paper.

Portable seats

It is possible to buy commercial seats from a range of companies. However, why not ask children to design and make a portable waterproof seat for using outside.

Set criteria such as:

- Size
- Being able to identify it
- Ease for carrying
- Small enough to store away

Simple solutions often work well, such as newspaper stuck in a bag. Old thermal sleeping mats or insulating bubble wrap (for sticking behind radiators) can be cut up and used too. However, bear in mind the following:

- Carpet tiles have their uses but aren't waterproof and take a long time to dry once wet; they are also cumbersome to carry. Remember, carpets are designed for indoors.
- Foam camping mats are available from outdoor shops, but check how robust they are before buying.

Clipboards

Different sizes of clipboard are really useful. Children seem to love little A5 clipboards. Any reluctant writers tend to perk up when they realise that extended writing is not going to happen outdoors (yet). A3 clipboards are great for sketching and artwork. They also work well for children with poor coordination skills because resting their elbows on the board gives them greater control when using pencils.

Light-coloured cloth

If natural objects, such as leaves and sticks, are placed on a light-coloured cloth (e.g. an old cotton sheet), then they are much easier to see and make a good focal point for discussions. The fabric has a multitude of other uses too, such as a cheap parachute, a sheet for catching bugs and beasties when placed under a tree, for playing memory games and so on.

Chalk

It helps to shop around for good deals on big chalks. Playgrounds often eat the stuff, so being conservative about its use can help. It is worth rummaging around in the backs of cupboards for old chalk from the days of blackboards. You may need to do a 'chalk talk' with your class prior to using it, as it is highly likely that at least one child will discover the fun of covering their hands with chalk and then going around patting others on the back. Interesting illustrations and words may also be chalked about the playground, so be vigilant!

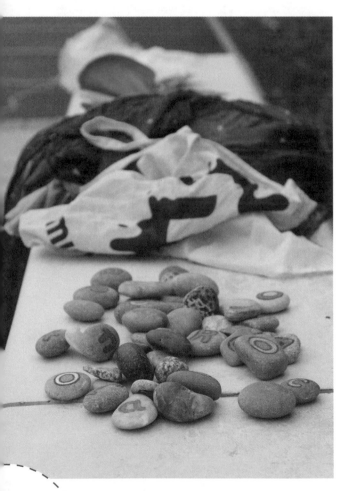

Magnifying glasses

Magnifying lenses are handy for looking at the world close up and in detail. I buy lots of assorted types of cheap magnifiers as different children find different lenses easier or harder to use.

Viewers

A viewer is just a homemade cardboard frame. You can make many different sorts. Wide frames allow more of the world to be seen and are suitable for looking at landscapes. Viewers with a small hole in the centre are useful for focusing on specific objects – toilet roll tubes also work well for this.

Natural materials

If your school grounds are full of trees, sand, stones and other natural materials then you may be teaching in outdoor heaven. If you only have asphalt, you may want to build up collections of sticks, stones, cones, leaves, shells and other similar items to use. Gather these sustainably in line with the access rights and laws in your country. Alternatively, purchase some natural materials, such as stones

and pebbles, from a DIY shop or building merchant. Advice on using sticks and stones with children is given in Chapter 11.

Digital equipment

Any digital equipment you use outside will need to be looked after carefully. Demonstrate and then allow the children to practise using each item before going out. Also include the storage and passing of items from one person to another, as this is when many objects are inadvertently dropped. It is worth investing in waterproof casings and robust covers which protect gear outdoors. Always ensure that the equipment is fully charged and you have spare batteries or items with you.

Identification guides

Children of all ages enjoy looking at identification books. The more opportunities they have to browse through these, inside and out, the more able they are to use them. Reluctant readers or children who are still learning to read can access ones with lots of photos or illustrations. Keep a few in the class library too. There is no need to spend a lot of money on these as there are many free or cheap ways of acquiring them:

- Download nature identification apps onto digital gadgets – there are small free versions. Remember to stick to your country.

- The Nature Detectives website is great for A4 pictorial guides.[6]

- Look in bargain bookshops for traditional field guides.

- Weekend newspapers sometimes have free guides.

- Second-hand guides can be picked up via Amazon or second-hand bookshops.

- The Field Studies Council has lots of laminated pictorial guides which can be bought through their website.[7]

If you are worried about your ability to identify plants and animals, have a look at the guidance in Chapter 11.

Idea 2.15 Ensure your children have suitable clothing and footwear

There is a lot of truth in the Scandinavian proverb, 'There's no such thing as bad weather, only bad clothing'. You and your class will have to learn to adapt to the climate and prevailing weather conditions. The more time spent outside, the more adept everyone will become at doing this.

If your school does not provide outdoor clothing or include this as part of the school uniform, then there are other options:

- Contact parents and carers. Let them know the class are doing lots of outdoor activities as part of the curriculum and could they remember to ensure their child has wellies, a jacket and, if possible, over-trousers too.

6 See <http://www.naturedetectives.org>
7 See <http://www.field-studies-council.org>

- Raid the lost property collection – see if you can find uncollected outdoor clothing.

- Visit charity shops and ask the volunteers to put aside outdoor clothing for your class. This is a time-consuming option but a lovely way of engaging the local community with your work and can lead to long-term relationships which work for the shops and the school.

- Ask for donations. This is another long-term option as you may only get a few, if any, from one request. It works best as an ongoing approach.

- Fundraise for a class set of clothes. First, get samples of outdoor clothing and find out which is the most popular. The class can rate the samples according to colour, texture, waterproof properties, ease of putting them on and taking them off, and so on.

- Make your own – challenge the class to design their own outdoor clothing from black bin liners and duct tape! This can be an ongoing design challenge for older classes.

Finally, be mindful about teaching children to assess the weather and their ability to cope. Encourage children to work out their own needs and decide what they ought to wear, rather than simply telling them to put on their jackets. In my experience, some children feel the cold more than others, and some children deal with hot weather better than others.

Getting everyone on board

Whilst research continues be published suggesting that learning outside is a very good thing in all sorts of ways, there are still the doubters. However, these people are your allies in disguise – use their concerns to your creative advantage.

Idea 2.16 The children who don't want to go outside

Children who do not want to go outside or struggle with outdoor activities are a useful baseline for looking at ways of improving your teaching techniques and the activities you are undertaking with your class.

There are many good reasons why children do not want to go outside and most of them are genuine. As a child, given a choice between playing inside and being outside, I would be indoors. At the age of six, I discovered that if I drank my milk really slowly, my 'punishment' was to stay inside at breaktime and wash out the milk bottles.

When I look back, the underlying reason for this dislike was feeling cold. I was often cold as a child and being outside made it worse. I grew up in the days where boys wore shorts all year round and girls wore miniskirts. I was bored from time to time as well.

My experiences of children today suggest they have similar reasons for not wanting to go out. For example, a child may say:

I hate being cold and get cold easily outside.

I don't have suitable clothing and won't be warm enough.

I prefer written work at a desk. (Going outside and doing practical activities puts them at a competitive disadvantage.)

I don't have choice in the matter. (The child feels powerless.)

I spend a lot of time outside and I need a break. (School gives them a break from being outside a lot.)

Being outside is boring.

I'm frightened. (This could be insects, other children, balls, open spaces, having an asthma attack or many other things.)

I don't like it. (It takes time to get used to working outside.)

Regardless of the reason, what is important is to chat with children and help them to work out solutions or coping mechanisms. For example, when working in one classroom, I found that offering a choice between indoor and outdoor activities worked well. Only once during the course of a year did a child actually opt to remain inside. With another child, the importance of being able to choose outdoor clothes to wear made a difference. He often used come to school without a sweatshirt or a jacket.

Idea 2.17 Reduce the possibility of parental complaints

Parents are generally overwhelmingly supportive of learning outside. Naturally, they need to be reassured that learning is going on and it's not all one big jolly. In my experience, if parents are invited to participate too, then they become strong advocates for outdoor activities. Nevertheless, here are some tips to consider:

■ Find out what your head teacher does and does not find acceptable before you embark on a regular commitment to learning outdoors. You need them on your side, so let them know about your plans and the benefits of your intended outdoor experiences.

■ Share your outdoor plans with parents and carers. Write this in a letter or, if necessary, have a meeting where they can ask questions and find out more. Again, focus on the benefits of learning outside.

■ Invite parents and carers to join you for an outdoor activity. This is an opportunity to demonstrate the quality of your outdoor work, have an extra helper to assist and share the joys of learning outside. If necessary, offer a general open invite.

■ Reassure parents that you are not the outdoor police. Their children's well-being, health and safety are of primary importance to you, along with their interest in, and engagement with, outdoor activities. Have alternative arrangements in place for truly inclement weather or demonstrate how you will switch around your timetable to accommodate bad weather.

■ Contribute to the school blog or create a class blog to record your outdoor activities. Again, keep the focus on the benefits of the work, what the children learned and photos and comments from the children themselves.

If a parent remains concerned

If parents are unconvinced, ask to make direct contact with them. Arrange a meeting, listen to what they have to say and take on board their concerns. Often there is a misunderstanding that needs to be cleared up.

For example, I once had a parent complain because her child was outside for PE lessons in February. Her child had asthma so understandably the parent was worried. It turned out she had not seen the letter about PE happening outside and did not know that her child could wrap up warmly. After some discussion, we agreed that the PE teacher would be asked to keep a close eye on her daughter's well-being and the parent would be contacted if there were any concerns.

Be gently assertive. Opting out of an activity should not normally be an option – it can create challenges of its own. The exceptions to this are where a fee may be charged for a special event, acts of religious observation or if a specific aspect of sex education takes place outside. In all such matters, follow your school policy.

Idea 2.18 Inform and reassure your head teacher

Head teachers and senior management teams are generally supportive of learning outside and most have been proactive in driving forward outdoor initiatives within their schools.

However, head teachers have to be able to justify everything which happens in their school. If something goes wrong, they suffer both personally and professionally. The stakes are high for them so, naturally, caution is needed.

To enable outdoor learning to happen, you may need to provide clear evidence and reassurance that:

■ The learning links into the rest of the work you have planned for the children.

■ The quality is at least as high as any indoor learning.

■ That you have undertaken appropriate risk–benefit assessments to enable the activities to happen safely.

■ That the children are enjoying the sessions and benefitting from learning outdoors.

■ That your outdoor experiences are a positive contribution to the life and ethos of the school.

This may sound like a tall order, but, just like every other activity you do, it is important for your line managers to know and understand what you are doing and why.

Idea 2.19 How much time should I be spending on learning outdoors?

My belief is that if a concept, skill or meaningful experience can be acquired outside, then we should make it happen there. I do not get hung up worrying about whether the indoors or outdoors is more 'appropriate'. It is like preparing a packed lunch for a child. You do not spend most of your time thinking about where your child will eat the lunch. Your focus is on providing a nutritious, balanced meal. If you know your child is going to be outside then you tweak the lunch appropriately. For example, you may provide hot soup in addition to a sandwich.

Teaching needs to be the same. Focus primarily on the quality of the learning, taking into account the place where it will happen, rather than the other way round. Teaching outside for the sake of it, because you have to spend X number of hours outside each week, is not good practice.

Often, the planned learning may work equally well inside or out. For example, many run-around maths activities could happen in a gym hall. This is great, in that if the weather is awful, the activity can be taught inside. However, if the children have the appropriate clothing and footwear, then it would be better if it takes place outside. These are sometimes referred to as 'place ambivalent' activities because being outside is not an essential requisite to the activity going ahead.

What is important to remember is that being outside for any activity offers benefits that indoor spaces do not. This is the unique and special nature of the outdoors, which provides:

- Fresh air
- Physical activity
- A feeling of space and freedom
- Learning how to cope in all weathers and seasons
- Natural light
- Access to nature (you will still find some even in urban environments)
- A change from being in the classroom
- Unexpected interactions (e.g. a plane flying overhead or a cat strolling by) which provide additional learning opportunities
- A greater range of multisensory experiences

Idea 2.20 How long should each outdoor session last?

Asking how long a session should last is akin to asking how long is a piece of string. It depends very much on a number of variables, such as the age of the children you teach, the ease of the planned learning for being taught outside, the weather and season, and whether your school has a conducive ethos in place. Avoid confusing quantity with quality.

37

If all your outdoor sessions simply involve a five-minute dash outside and then back in, it is questionable as to how much learning is actually happening outside.

A rough timescale may look like this:

- Running outside to quickly find an item or take photos.

- Going outside for a short game or activity as part of a longer session which includes indoor work before and/or afterwards.

- Undertaking a session outside with several activities taking place.

- Spending a half day undertaking an outdoor activity.

- A full day outside, perhaps an off-site visit.

- A residential experience involving overnight stays.

- An outdoor school where as much learning as possible takes place outside all year round in all weathers – the indoors is a last rather than a first resort.

Common sense says that in the warmer months, more outdoor sessions are likely to happen, with longer amounts of time spent outside. However, aim to be outside at least weekly all year round so that you and your class develop the habit of working outside.

Idea 2.21 There isn't enough time for outdoor learning

Most practitioners who tell me that there isn't enough time for outdoor learning are treating 'outdoor learning' as a subject. The trick is to look at your planned learning for the week and consider what would best be taught as an outdoor session. For example, you may decide to focus on maths and, once a week, have a whole-class outdoor session that is used to recap basic concepts and facts. Art and PE activities naturally lend themselves to outdoor work. Many science and social studies lessons also work well outside. It is worthwhile developing a series of lessons within a curriculum area that can be easily adapted and used again.

Remember to keep your outdoor sessions snappy. Develop routines with your class so that they are on-task quickly and the amount of dead time is minimised. See Chapter 3 for some suggestions.

Idea 2.22 The 'challenging' class of children

It can be daunting taking any class outside. When you have children who present particularly challenging behaviour, either collectively or individually, it can feel extra scary.

Many children think that the playground is *their* space. They can sometimes believe that being outside is all about playing. This means that, even during class time, it can take a while before a child understands that specific tasks can be expected of them outside. This will change over time, so it is worth persevering. Children do get used to learning outside.

Often, it is the children who exhibit the most challenging behaviour indoors that can benefit most from spending time learning outside. They enjoy the freedom and space. The multisensory nature of being outside can help to improve understanding. Not needing to read or write can boost confidence. Practical lessons can be easier to understand. Overall, children tend to feel more relaxed outside.

Other useful strategies include:

- If your school has a behaviour policy, make it clear to all children that this applies outside too. There is no difference between indoors and out.

- Be firm, fair and consistent. This may sound obvious but often this inadvertently causes resentment if children think they are not being treated fairly and equitably.

- Make your outdoor learning captivating. If the children are not interested and engaged, they are less likely to behave. As always, learning needs to be challenging, relevant and fun.

- Follow advice from behaviour specialists. There are many effective techniques which work just as well in outdoor contexts.

If you have a child with additional support needs, then it is worth looking at their individual risk assessment and considering what strategies and support may be required to enable them to successfully access outdoor opportunities. For example, a child may be happier going outside if he or she is allowed to take their favourite soft toy.

Before You Go Outside checklist

Have you:

- ■ Read this book!

- ■ Got suitable clothing and footwear for yourself?

- ■ Planned outdoor experiences which are fully integrated into your curriculum and not an add-on? Aim for one activity per week to begin with.

- ■ Discussed your plans with your line manager/head teacher?

- ■ Talked with your class about why you are going to be learning outside?

- ■ Informed parents of your plans?

- ■ Briefed any other adults who may be working with you?

- ■ Walked the school boundary and around your local area and found out what is outside? Do you know what natural materials and other objects are readily available?

- ■ Gathered any resources that you think you may need?

- ■ Checked the school policy about collecting materials in the grounds? If none exists, discuss this with your head teacher. If necessary, start collecting in a sustainable manner in line with the access rights in your country.

- ■ Worked out how you are getting your class outside and where the exit/entrances are so children can nip to the toilet if necessary?

- ■ Created a risk–benefit assessment which includes meeting the specific needs of any children with particular needs?

CHAPTER 3

The First Few Sessions

This chapter is about getting started. The first few times you take your class outside, the overarching aim will be to acclimatise to the process. It is about putting routines and expectations in place around learning outside.

If it is the start of a new school year, then take your class outside from the beginning. This means that the children get used to being outside as part of being in your class. In my experience, it is much easier than waiting a month or two before venturing out – and the weather is still nice and warm.

If you are halfway through the academic year, be prepared for children to be initially more unsettled. Change sometimes takes time to embed.

Indoor routines to get outside

Actually getting outdoors can be one of the hardest aspects of going outside to learn. Transitions between activities often need a bit of attention to ensure a smooth changeover. A little practice and fine-tuning is normal when children are getting used to working outside.

Idea 3.1 Make lining up a challenge

Lining up works well as a class challenge. At the beginning, discuss tactics for ensuring everyone gets outside with the minimum of fuss. Ask the class to consider:

- Why is it worthwhile getting outside quickly and quietly?
- What will we need to do to ensure this happens (e.g. go to toilet, wash hands, pick up clothes, change shoes, collect equipment, line up)?
- What will we see and hear if this works well?
- How long do we think this will take us?

Once children are lined up, have a quick review of how the class got on. Ask them to think about what worked well and what could be even better the next time. Note the suggestions and, at the next outdoor session, remind the class to try out their ideas. This sets in motion the review–plan–do process.

Have high expectations of your class, regardless of the children's age. Eventually, you can reach a situation where children can simply get up and go without any ado. In one Seattle infant school that I visited, the children disappeared in less than one minute when my back was turned to look at a wall display. I did not even hear them leave. When I found the class outside, they were all lying on their backs looking up at the trees.

Useful things to consider:

- If your class has an outside door, then look at the opportunities for free-flow learning between the classroom and the immediate space outside. See Idea 11.3 for more on this.

- Meet children in the playground after an interval or lunchtime so there is no need to go inside.

- Reorganise your indoor space so that the few outdoor resources required are immediately to hand and not locked in a cupboard at the other end of the school.

Idea 3.2 Ambulatory activities

Ambulatory activities are those which happen on the move. If you are in a classroom that requires a bit of walking to get out of the building, then try to make this time part of the session (if it fits with the rest of your planned activities). For example:

- Can the children move along the corridor and outside in different ways (e.g. tiptoe like a mouse, stride like a giant, amble like an elephant).
- Do a chant or sing a song at the same time.
- Step on every tile in a line (if you have a tiled corridor).
- Walk like soldiers – great for the Romans or other historical projects.
- Play follow my leader – with everyone copying the actions of the person at the front of the line.

Remind children to keep doing the ambulatory activity until they reach the gathering circle (see Idea 3.3). Otherwise, most children will get to the outside door and … run!

If children are full of energy, then getting them to run to the end of the playing field and back to the circle can be a good energy burner. With high-octane classes, you will need to experiment with ways of getting them to calm down. Sometimes, a short meditation exercise or mindfulness activity can help. Have a look at the ideas in Chapter 4.

Outside with the class

Idea 3.3 Create a gathering place

Just like indoors, it is good to have a place to come together as a class. A gathering circle is a lovely way of building a collaborative, shared learning experience. A circle lends itself naturally to discussions, reflections and reviewing tasks, as well as games and action activities. It is also a throwback to generations gone by when communities would gather around a fire to share food, tell stories and develop bonds of friendship.

The first time you take a class outside, it is worthwhile spending time getting children used to gathering and doing circle-based activities. This helps children understand that it is different to playtime. It is also an opportunity to review ground rules and behaviour expectations. The circle can become a unique and special part of being outside.

Gathering circles can be:

- A circle or series of concentric rings painted on the playground. They make good guidelines for young children who are learning what making a circle is all about.
- A temporary circle created by portable seats or a rope to mark the edge. Chalk can also be used to draw a circle.
- Anywhere the class can make a circle that is fit for purpose. This can be very useful when out and about or for getting together in different parts of the school grounds.
- Fixed seats or logs in a circle.

It is best to experiment with temporary circles first, so that you and the children find the best place outside. It also means children can be properly involved in the process. This is important: they are being asked to sit there and learn, so they need a design which suits their needs.

Note: The sun is a welcome addition to any outdoor activity. When standing in the gathering circle, make sure that you face the sun rather than the children – otherwise, they find it hard to look at you and concentrate. If you need to wear sunglasses, check that you can still make eye contact.

Gathering tips and tricks

Being able to call children back to the circle is a valuable time-saver and keeps activities flowing smoothly. It can take practise, so try some of these approaches.

Idea 3.4 Establish a gathering call and signal

The children can devise calls and experiment to find out which one can be heard best outside. Often one that changes pitch works well. Test different noise-makers, such as whistles and drums, or invent ones to save shouting.

Alternatively, use a gathering signal – sometimes it is easier being seen than heard. See what actions your class think are most effective.

Idea 3.5 Time the class making a perfect gathering circle

Ask the children what a good gathering circle will look like. Draw up criteria so that your class aim to get a decent shape each time as quickly as possible. Next, increase the challenge – can the class remember their position in the circle and line up correctly? What happens if you move the gathering circle to different places?

Idea 3.6 Sticky circles

The sticky circle is a useful alternative to asking children to hold hands when making a circle. When you call out:

- 'Sticky feet' the children need to ensure their feet are touching those of the two people standing either side of them.
- 'Sticky elbows' involves putting hands on hips and having elbows touching.
- 'Sticky tips' is standing with arms outstretched and fingertips touching.
- 'Sticky shoulders' is a group huddle – do this on cold, windy days so that you can hear each other speak more easily. The sound seems to get magnified slightly in a tight circle.

You could also play Simon says or similar games to get children tuned into the different commands and adjusting the size of the circle.

Circle time

If your class has regular circle times, then use this approach outside too. It can be a familiar framework which will help children acclimatise to formal learning outside. Many circle time activities can be adapted for outside. Stories, especially fables, legends and folk tales also lend themselves to being told or dramatised outdoors. Here is a selection of activities that I commonly use.

Idea 3.7 Circle pass

Equipment: A range of balls of different sizes and weights

Everyone kneels in a circle facing inwards and passes the ball from person to person using a flat, open hand (palm up). When first learning the game, it is easier for the children to use two flat hands side-by-side rather than one. The object is to move the ball around the circle as rapidly as possible without actually grasping it. If it is dropped, simply pick it up and begin passing again. Challenge the class to go around the circle faster with each new start. Very young children find it hard not to grasp a ball, so using a big one can help.

Idea 3.8 Circle the circle

Equipment: Several hoops and a stopwatch

In a circle, everyone holds hands. A hoop is passed around the circle by each person stepping through the hoop and moving it onto the next person without letting go of their hands. This activity can be timed, with the class aiming to get the hoop passed around the circle as quickly as possible. More hoops can be added into the circle and passed around to keep everyone busy. The fun really begins when the hoops are sent in opposite directions and have to cross over!

Idea 3.9 Follow my leader

The class sits in a circle and a child is chosen to be the detective. He or she turns their back to the group and closes their eyes whilst a leader is chosen. The leader then begins an action which the rest of the class copies (e.g. clapping hands in rhythm). The detective opens their eyes, turns around and begins looking for the leader. When the detective isn't looking, the leader changes to another mime (e.g. combing their hair) and everyone else follows suit. The detective has to work out who is the leader as the actions continue to change.

Idea 3.10 Circle slap

The circle slap needs to take place on smooth dry surfaces. Have everyone lie on their stomachs in a circle facing into the centre. Each person's arms should cross over the arms of the two people on either side of them. Everyone should have their palms touching the floor – this will form a circle of hands. A player is chosen to start the game. They lift their right hand up off the ground and slap it down. The hand that comes next in the circle (and therefore should slap next) is the left hand of the second person to the right of the starter. Then the right hand of the person next to the starter slaps and the slapping continues around the circle in order. The challenge is to complete a circle of slaps in the correct order in the fastest time. Once the children have got the idea extra rules can be added, such as, at any time, someone may slap twice which means that the slapping should switch directions.

Idea 3.11 Fox and squirrels

Equipment: Three soft balls, two of them should be similar (for the foxes) and a smaller one for the squirrel

The aim of the game is for the foxes to catch the squirrel by tagging whoever is holding the squirrel ball with one (or both) of the fox balls. Everyone stands in a circle and begins passing the fox balls from player to player. Encourage the group to work at top speed and suggest that they reverse the direction of travel. Next introduce the squirrel ball. Whilst the fox balls may only be passed around the circle from one person to the next, the squirrel ball can be thrown across the circle. Encourage the children to call out 'fox' or 'squirrel' every time they pass one of the balls. Whilst there may be sympathy for the squirrel, it is not always the favourite with all children. Some might become fox sympathisers who choose to toss the squirrel to the foxes!

Idea 3.12 Everybody up

Get the class to sit down facing inwards and holding hands. On the count of three, everyone should try to stand up without breaking hands.

Idea 3.13 Team challenges and games

Team challenges can be adapted and put into most contexts or projects, so this is worthwhile doing to increase the relevance of the work. For some ideas, have a look at Adam Fletcher and Kari Kunst's booklet, *Guide to Cooperative Games for Social Change*.[1]

Moving away from the gathering circle

The next step is to introduce activities which involve children moving away from the gathering circle and coming back. You may wish to identify clear working boundaries – for example, children must always be able to see you or perhaps they should stay within the playground rather than going onto the playing field.

The suggestions below are just for starters. Challenge children to come up with their own variations or ideas too.

---

1 A. Fletcher and K. Kunst, *Guide to Cooperative Games for Social Change* (Olympia, WA: CommonAction), 2006. Available at: <http://www.commonaction.org/gamesguide.pdf>

Idea 3.14 Run and touch

Call out instructions such as 'Run and touch something … green … rough and flat … you can sit on … natural … man-made …' and so on. After each instruction, call the class back to the gathering circle. Time them, if necessary, to see how quickly they can return. Ask the children to call out their ideas too. You will discover some wonderful divergent thinking!

Idea 3.15 Stone hunt

Pass around a bag of stones and ask each child to take one. When you give the signal, the children have to run and put the stone somewhere and come back to the circle. Count to ten so that the children are encouraged to put the stones down and come back quickly. The next part is to challenge the children to find a different stone to their original one and to bring it back to the circle. How quickly can the class do this? What strategies are worth trying? This activity may take several attempts before a solution is found.

The next challenge is being able to return the stone to its original owner within the shortest time frame. How can this be achieved? Is it possible for a class to undertake this activity in silence?

Idea 3.16 Stone angels

Ask all the children to take ten big steps away from the gathering circle and stand still. Then challenge them to creep back to the circle without you seeing them move. You cover up your eyes, but the moment you uncover them, the children must stand absolutely still. If you see them move, they must sit down. Is it possible for the whole class to get back to the circle? When children freeze, encourage them to look like the scary weeping angels seen in *Doctor Who*.

Idea 3.17 Moving about games

It is quite likely that your class will have experience of doing PE or physical games and activities outside. So, beginning with activities that involve a lot of moving about and action help them tune into learning outside in ways that are already familiar to them.

Your class will probably know several suitable games. These can be played outside whilst you all get used to being there. A useful source of games, stories and activities can be found on the Ultimate Camp Resource website.[2]

Find something interesting

One of the challenges of working with a new class is learning how to engage them. Most classes have children from many different backgrounds and with a diverse spread of interests and abilities.

'Find something interesting' is a good starting point for demonstrating that the environment itself is the main resource and stimulus for learning outside. When we challenge children to 'find something interesting', we are asking them to select and use moveable materials that are available in the environment.

Many objects lying around outside have a lot of educational potential, particularly natural resources such as sticks, stones, leaves, common weeds and seeds. They are open-ended materials with no fixed or defined purpose, unlike many bought education resources. This means that children can use them in many creative and imaginative ways.

For example, if you watch a child playing with a toy car, it is very likely that the car will be used as a car. It may become a Batmobile or a turbo-charged super-car but it is still a car. If a child picks

---

2 See <http://www.ultimatecampresource.com>

up a stick, however, it may become a gun, or a fishing rod or a wand. So the open-endedness of a stick, or its 'affordance', is much higher.

Idea 3.18 The potential of a stick

This is an activity for you, but you could also try it out with your class. Find a toy car and a stick. Spend one minute writing down or brainstorming ideas about how a child might use the car when playing. Next, do the same with the stick. Then compare the ideas.

Which object results in a greater number of uses? Which object changes and becomes different things? What does this say about the play value of each object? How can these concepts be transferred to a teaching activity?

The versatility of natural resources comes into formal learning opportunities too. When we ask children to 'find something interesting', we are making the most of the creative potential of natural resources for educational purposes.

Many children lack knowledge about the natural world around them. Yet, when asked to 'find something interesting', many children will bring back a natural object such as a stick, stone or common weed. When children choose an object, a bond is created and the children are beginning to connect in a very real way to their environment. At the very least, they will have had to look around and make a decision. There is also a curiosity which comes into the session as the children have no idea how they will be asked to use their object.

The 'find something interesting' approach works in most outdoor spaces or natural environments, so it can be used for spontaneous or planned activities in a park, on a beach or in the school grounds. This also means that comparisons can be made between different places – for example, a storytelling session in woodland using found objects will be very different to one in the school grounds.

The 'find something interesting' quest is a year-round all-weather activity, although there is no need to stay outside if the children are cold, wet or uncomfortable. Once the objects have been found, the follow-up can happen inside if there is no suitable shelter outside and the weather is inclement.

I often ask classes of children to 'find something interesting' and bring it back to the gathering circle. It is useful technique for introducing parameters and boundaries without sounding like a health and safety officer with compulsive tendencies! The trick is to ask the children if there is anything they should not bring back to the gathering circle, and why, before they dash off. The responses are almost always sensible, such as 'sharp objects', 'dirty stuff' and 'live animals'.

You may wish to put a size guide on the request too. In the past I've had children who have brought back a range of assorted finds including fence posts (passed on to the school janitor after the outdoor session), large rocks, an uprooted holly tree and large branches.

You need to have a plan for the gathered objects once the session is finished. You may decide to put back the objects in the same place you found them, place any litter gathered in a bin, take broken objects to the janitor to be fixed or bring objects into class for follow-up work and display purposes.

With big or unsettled classes, I may ask trios of children to find one object collectively. This can encourage children to work together and negotiate.

Once each child has found an object and brought it back to the gathering circle, there are a range of different activities which work well. Below is just a small smattering of the possibilities.

Idea 3.19 Ask a question

Each child or trio needs to think for a moment and write down a question about their individual object. Go round the circle and request that each question is asked as the object is put into the centre of the circle. The questions do not need to be answered there and then – sometimes it is better to have a pause for thought.

This can lead into lots of discussions about:

- What makes a good question: open-ended ones or closed ones?
- Are there connections between any questions (e.g. their structure or their theme)?
- What's the point of asking and thinking up questions?

This can then lead onto further explorations and games outside in subsequent sessions, such as twenty questions (Idea 3.20) or Leonardo da Vinci's curiosity challenge (Idea 4.14).

Idea 3.20 Twenty questions

It is possible to play variations of guessing games using the objects the children have collected. This works well in encouraging children to ask a question that gives them the answer they are looking for! One child should silently choose one of the objects brought to the gathering circle. The other children then take turns asking a question which helps everyone to work out which object is the chosen one. The responder can only answer 'yes', 'no' or 'don't know'. A direct question may only be asked three times (e.g. 'Is it the buttercup?').

Once the children know how to play this game, they can work in smaller groups or pairs and do this as a finishing-off activity.

Idea 3.21 Leaf line-up

This activity provides a way of introducing rules about gathering materials outside. It is up to your school to discuss and agree a policy about this. If you have a large school, 500 children working outside could easily strip the bushes bare! It may be prudent for the children to only collect fallen leaves, dead material or common weeds. Alternatively, other materials, such as stones, can be substituted.

Ask the children to find a leaf each and bring it back to the circle. After this, request that they arrange themselves in order around the circle so that the person with the smallest leaf stands on your left and the person with the largest leaf stands on your right. If you listen, all sorts of mathematical discussions will take place as well as decision-making over the criteria. Should the stem be included? Is it the width or the length of leaf which counts?

For younger children, this activity can be completed by the children taking it in turns to put the leaf down in a line from smallest to largest in the circle. This allows for more shared discussions. On a windy day, stones may be needed to keep the leaves in place. Alternatively, use sticks instead of leaves.

Idea 3.22 Getting it sorted

When the children have brought their object to the gathering circle, ask them to put it on a piece of light-coloured cloth in the centre of the circle and silently sort the objects by colour. Challenge the class to work out how you are sorting them. Then ask the children to think about how the materials could be sorted in other ways and invite them to take turns to arrange the materials (e.g. by size, living and non-living, shape, weight, rough and smooth).

From here, introduce Venn diagrams or Carroll diagrams to further classify the materials. The children can work in pairs or small groups to create a diagram – they may need to find more interesting objects to do this. Use hoops for Venn diagrams and sticks or chalk to create Carroll diagrams.

Idea 3.23 There's angles everywhere

Separate the found objects according to the angles identified. For example, a block of wood or an empty crisp packet will contain right angles, whilst leaves often have examples of acute angles in their veins.

What can the children deduce from this evidence? Are there more right angles to be found in man-made objects than in natural ones? How can this theory be proved? From here, an angle hunt can take place within a designated area.

Idea 3.24 The same and different game

At the gathering circle, ask the children to pair off with the person beside them. Each pair looks at their objects and asks, 'What's the same about these things?' and 'What's different?' They must come up with two or three similarities and differences. This activity helps children look closely at objects to distinguish key characteristics and features.

Idea 3.25 Why five?

Why five? is a useful development from Idea 3.24 and takes its inspiration from the fact that many inventors and designers look at ideas from one system or area and apply them to another.

The found objects are compared in groups of up to five children. The group has to come up with a chain of five connections between the objects. For example:

1   Birch leaf – this can be found at the end of a living branch, which, when it dies becomes a stick.

2   Stick – a stick is a dead branch upon which a pine cone once grew.

3   Pine cone – as the scales of the cone dry out, they open up, releasing the seeds which are distributed by the wind.

4   Dandelion – also relies on wind dispersal of its seeds. If you blow hard enough on a dande-lion clock, the seeds disperse in an explosion of fluff.

5   Lichen – this is fluffy and soft to feel and can be found growing on birch trees.

Idea 3.26 The biography of an object

The children should find someone with a similar or the same object. Together, they invent a brief biography or life history of the object using a maximum of five sentences. For example:

> My dandelion was born from a seed that landed on the playing field. It nestled into the ground one late spring day and immediately began sprouting. Within a week the dandelion had put down a strong tap root. Within a month it had grown a beautiful golden head. Then I picked it.

> My wrapper was created with a purpose – to protect the Mars bar from the dangers in its life. It encased the snack bar and they lived happily together for several months on a shop shelf. One day, a boy bought the Mars bar. Without caring one jot, he tore the wrapper off the sweet and chucked it into the wind. I found it sheltering in the corner of the playground.

Back in the classroom, these biographies can be written into miniature books and placed beside each object on a display table.

Idea 3.27 Symbols and map making

If a gathering circle happens on asphalt, then a class-sized map can be created from the found objects. Have a discussion about what the objects could represent. Ask the children to arrange the objects in an interesting way to create a territory, land or country. For example, a big rock might be a mountain. The weeds might be a meadow. A piece of old blue rope might be a river.

Once the 3D map has been created, use chalk to carefully draw round or under each object. Next, remove the objects – their outline will remain on the ground. With very young children, they can take turns to guess and put the objects back onto the 2D outlines. With older children, you could discuss various features of maps, such as how to annotate them correctly, the purpose and use of a key and so on.

After this sort of activity, children will very often want to go and make their own miniature versions nearby. This can be an ideal springboard into writing about the landscape.

Idea 3.28 The rhythm of words

All words have a rhythm which helps us to understand how they are constructed. Ask children to think about their object and describe it. For very young children, a simple description may be enough (e.g. green grass, long stick, tickly feather). With older children, you might ask for alliteration, the creation of a simile or the invention of a plural noun or a metaphor.

Once the children have made up their descriptive words or phrases, it is time to get the rhythms going. In turn, each child tells the class their description. The class must repeat the description and, at the same time, clap the rhythm out loud. For example:

- Green grass   2 syllables = 2 claps
- Long stick   2 syllables = 2 claps
- Tickly feather   4 syllables = 4 claps

If the children get tired of clapping, then snapping their fingers, slapping their thighs, stamping their feet or jumping up and down work well too.

A greater challenge is to break a phrase into its syllables with each child in turn clapping just once. For example, tickly feather would be clapped by four children in turn, each saying aloud their part of the phrase:

tick (clap)   ly (clap)   fea (clap)   ther (clap)

From here, syllable poems can be developed, such as a haiku or tanka.

The First Few Sessions checklist

Have you:

- ■ Decided your line-up routine with the children and how you are going to exit the school?

- ■ Chosen a suitable gathering place and activities that will help children gather there quickly?

- ■ Put together a few circle games, familiar games and activities that you and your children already know, such as traditional playground games? Think about how these could be adapted to class interests and themes and used during outside sessions or for outdoor circle times.

- ■ Planned a series of outdoor sessions based on the ideas in this chapter and elsewhere? Aim for at least one outdoor session per week.

- ■ Planned how this will be followed up back in class or the next time you are outside?

- ■ Have alternative indoor activities ready, if needed?

CHAPTER 4

Thinking, Reflecting and Reviewing

In the previous chapter, we concentrated on whole-class activities using a gathering circle as the main focal point. In this chapter, we extend working outside to activities where children may be working on their own and, at times, away from the gathering circle. These are assignments that involve thinking and reflecting, and often require physical space and a time set aside for this purpose.

As much as possible, try to link these activities into ongoing themes and projects, rather than treating them as isolated activities.

Time to be alone

Whilst children thrive working in groups and learning together, there is also a need for them to learn how to work by themselves outside. The space and freedom afforded by the outdoors can give children a sense of calm and peace. With most of the activities in this chapter, your class may need a couple of attempts to get tuned into being quiet and benefitting from the experience. Often it is good to begin with a hiding game. This helps children keep quiet outside for a clear, fun purpose!

When explaining the activities, make sure you clarify the physical boundaries – for example, you may wish to request that the children remain within a certain area of the school grounds. This can stop the temptation to try and hide in the car park around the corner!

Idea 4.1 Sardines

For younger children, sardines works well if there is another adult present or an older child. One adult goes and hides. After counting to fifty, the children have to hunt for the hidden adult. When a child finds the adult, he or she must sit or lie down beside them and wait silently for others to come and join them. Eventually all the class will be there. On the count of three, everyone shouts 'Sardines!' and gets up. The game can be repeated – perhaps one or two children could hide together for everyone else to find.

Idea 4.2 Sound 'n' seek

This is a game for older children, which is an adaptation of sardines (Idea 4.1), where the children work in teams.

- Each team chooses a name and devises a victory chant (e.g. 'We are the knights of the round table … Young, fit and very able').

- Each team needs one person to be the 'keeper of the sound'. This person has two pebbles. Using the pebbles, they must devise a group rhythm through tapping them together.

- Check each group thoroughly knows their victory chant and recognises their pebble rhythm, which must be different for each group.

The keeper of the sound for each group goes off and hides out of sight in a particular area – each keeper needs to be away from the others. After one minute, the rest of the class goes into the designated area. They have to move quietly so that they can hear the pebble rhythm of their team. When they find their keeper of the sound, the children must sit silently beside them. Once all members of the team have found the keeper of the sound, the team can give their victory chant. The first team to do this wins. The game can be repeated with amendments suggested by the class and a discussion about which strategies which work best.

Idea 4.3 Far apart

What is the furthest apart each person in the class can sit from each other whilst still see the teacher and vice versa? Give your class this challenge:

- How long do they think it will take them to work this out?

- How will they measure the distances they are spaced out from each other?

- Does it work best if they aim for a pattern, such as everyone being exactly one metre from another person?

Idea 4.4 Solitude mapping

Ask children to mark on a map of the school grounds the best place for being alone. This can be helpful for identifying where to go when doing an activity which requires a bit of space or solitude.

If your school is lucky enough to have plenty of space or a nearby woodland site, then the opportunity to create individual dens as a place of sanctuary, and also to work alone, is not to be missed. See Chapter 5 for den building ideas.

Idea 4.5 A reflective walk

This activity works well if children struggle to separate from each other outside.

Explain to the children that they are going to walk in a single line slowly and quietly, each carrying their portable seat. When you give a nod to the person at the front of the line, they must sit down at that spot and not say a word. If they wish, they can close their eyes. A short while further on, you should indicate for the next child to sit down. This continues until you have placed all the children around the edge of the playing field, school boundary or whatever area you are using, where they are far enough apart not to disturb each other.

Then proceed to collect each child in order. One by one, as you pass each child, they should silently join the line. Once all the children have been collected, move back to the gathering place. Then ask the children to have a discussion:

■ What happened or what did you notice when sitting alone?

■ Did anyone find it a positive experience? If so, how?

■ Did anyone find it challenging or difficult? If so, in what way?

■ How did it feel sitting alone?

■ What would you change about the activity to improve it?

■ What did you think about?

■ Have you ever done anything similar?

Idea 4.6 Stone meditation

If your class has practised mindfulness or undertaken meditation activities indoors, then these can be adapted for being outside. For example, challenge the children to find a stone and bring it to the gathering circle. They should sit facing outwards and spend a minute examining their stone silently, before turning back in and discussing their thoughts.

Idea 4.7 Finding your special place

This activity is useful for developing reflective time and working alone outdoors with children. It is also a good place to go to undertake solitary activities. A 'magic spot' is a special place in the school grounds or local wood that children recognise as their own. It will be at least a double arm's length away from another person.

Begin by asking the children to look at the patterns on their hand – they should have a good look at the palm lines, knuckle lines, fingerprints and other unique features. Challenge each child to find a pattern somewhere within a designated space outside which matches or resembles one of the patterns they have observed on their hand. It could be:

- A root pattern on the ground.
- Branches in a tree (they should sit underneath rather than in them!).
- A crack in a wall or concrete.
- A trail left by a snail.
- Sticks on the ground.

Once the children have found their pattern in the environment, they should sit there. Some children may take a while, in which case they might have to search over several sessions until they find a special place. Begin by asking them to sit silently for a minute and build this up slowly.

Idea 4.8 Sounds of silence

Sounds of silence is a good scene-setting activity for looking at silent letters in words. Agree with your class before beginning the activity which is the quietest part of the school grounds or outdoor space. Can the children go and sit there silently? Is it possible for them to move quietly without making a sound as you journey there?

At the gathering place, make a list of silent sounds (e.g. a spider weaving a web, the wind gently blowing on one's face). The children have to write or draw their ideas in silence.

After several minutes, get the children to read out their favourite idea from their own list. Have a moment's pause between each child's statement to emphasise the silence between each one. As the children do this, record their ideas to create a class poem of 'The Sounds of Silence' using a digital voice recorder.

Back inside, ask each child to choose a text and find the words which contain silent sounds. For example, 'ghost' contains the silent letter 'h'. Alternatively, you can provide texts for different groups based upon their ability. From the words and silent letters identified, can the children see letter patterns for silent sounds (e.g. -mb in thumb).

Listening and other sensory activities

Sensory activities can be introduced to give children something to focus on or think about when they are outside. They can be super springboards into literacy or art activities undertaken outside or back in class.

Idea 4.9 Sound maps

Create a map of sounds which can be heard in front, behind, to the left and the right. These can be words, symbols or pictures, depending on age and ability. The sounds can be linked to compass directions too.

Idea 4.10 Cloud watching

Get the children to lie back and watch the clouds. Then ask them to draw the shapes and pictures they see. Perhaps the clouds make pictures, but what about the blue sky in-between – the negative space? Encourage them to practise vaporising a cloud – making it disappear by removing it from their thoughts.

Idea 4.11 Idea trees

Idea trees is a useful finishing-off activity. The children should sit under a tree and wait for a good idea to pop into their head – the Buddha drew inspiration from Bhodi trees and an apple fell on Newton's head! Have sticky notes or paper to hand to write down the good ideas that emerge. The ideas do not have to be about any particular subject, unless you want to use this activity within a specific theme or project.

Idea 4.12 Watch the leaves wave

Watching waving leaves can be done by asking the children to lie on their backs under a tree and look up. Alternatively, they could look in a small mirror placed on the ground in front of where they are sitting and enjoy the reflection of the leaves and branches.

Idea 4.13 The exact spot

Provide a simple cardboard viewing frame. Ask the children to put it on a patch of ground in front of them and focus on the ground it frames. They should study it for a few minutes. When the children are back in the gathering circle, have a discussion about what their spot reminded them of and whether they will ever find this exact place again. If so, how?

Group thinking activities

Most of the suggestions below aim to encourage children to think and to enjoy the process of thinking. By working with others, ideas can be shared and enjoyed.

Idea 4.14 Leonardo da Vinci's curiosity challenge

Leonardo strongly believed in the value of curiosity. He understood that asking questions is more important than being able to answer them, as it leads to new ideas and ways of thinking.

Working in pairs, challenge your class to walk around outside and write or record with a digital recorder as many questions as they possibly can in the space of ten minutes. They can be questions linked to what they see, hear, feel and smell outside. They may also be random questions which pop into their heads based on how they are feeling. This helps out the reluctant writers who can then question the purpose of the activity (e.g. 'Why do I have to do this task?' or 'Isn't there anything better to do with my time?').

After the question compilation activity, the children can work through their lists and identify their three favourite questions. From here, discussions can be had about what makes a good question as well as how the activity helped them to explore their environment.

Edinburgh University outdoor lecturer, Simon Beames, has developed a flexible project called Outdoor Journeys, which starts with a question.[1] It provides a useful model for exploring your local area, particularly within specific subjects or projects.

Idea 4.15 Think laterally

This activity takes lateral thinking outside. There is a popular game where one child reads out a statement and, through questioning, the other children deduce what the situation is. The person presenting the situation may only answer 'yes', 'no', 'don't know' or 'irrelevant'. For example:

- A man pushes a car to a hotel. He pays £200 and pushes the car away again. (Answer: It is a game of Monopoly.)

- The window is open. The curtain is blowing. Ant and Dec lie dead on the floor in a puddle of water and broken glass. (Answer: Ant and Dec are goldfish. A gust of wind knocked their bowl onto the floor.)

Split the class into groups and encourage them to brainstorm ideas about the statement they have been given. Take a question from each group in turn until the puzzle is worked out.

A similar approach can be taken outside. Working in small groups, the children have to create a statement based upon a scenario observed outside for others to investigate through asking questions. For example:

Statement: In the middle of nowhere, the tracks disappeared.

Scenario: A bird walking along the ground flies off when it sees a cat in the distance.

---

1 See <http://outdoorjourneys.org.uk>

Idea 4.16 Everything is useful

Use the 'find something interesting' approach to ask children to gather materials outside. Working in groups, the children should brainstorm as many different uses for their gathered objects as they can within a given period of time. This can be followed up inside by researching what products or uses have been developed from their object. For example, juice cartons can be recycled into place mats and dandelion roots make a coffee substitute.

Idea 4.17 Science I-spy

In a gathering circle, take turns to play 'I spy with my little eye, an example of science beginning with …' Initially the children may struggle to think of examples but once they grasp the range of possibilities, they will flourish. For example:

- R is for roots – part of the structure of a plant.
- S is for sun – which gives us energy.
- D is for decay – which is what happens when a plant dies.

Idea 4.18 Nim

Nim is an ancient game of mathematical strategy. Strategy games are great ways of encouraging strategic thinking and planning ahead. They are also played in various forms around the world, so this makes a lovely partnership project with a school in a different country.

Nim is usually played in pairs. Each pair needs to collect twenty stones, cones or other small objects to use as counters. Taking turns, each player chooses to pick up one, two or three counters. The player who picks up the last counter loses the game.

Once the children are familiar with Nim, encourage them to look for patterns and strategic approaches to playing. Begin with a few investigative questions such as:

- There is a trick you can use to ensure you do not lose – can you discover it?
- What happens if three people take turns to play instead of two? How can a player apply the secret strategy?
- What happens if you change the number of pebbles used?
- What other investigations into pattern and probability can you make?

Idea 4.19 Scenes of death and decay

Late autumn and winter are ideal times to explore death and decay. Trees lose their leaves, wild-flowers are dying and the amount of dead and dying matter accumulates. It can offer a gentle approach to discussing death in the context of the natural world.

Ask the children to collect small examples of death and decay. If they are each given a small flat tile of soft clay, they can press their found items into this and leave them to air dry. Children can then have fun trying to identify the different parts of plants and plant species from the impressions.

A useful follow-up is to ask the children to read about Hades, the Greek god who ruled the underworld. Ask the class to imagine what Hades' underworld might be like. From here each child could create a little underworld scene made only from dead or dying material. This works best on bare soil. See if the children can work out why – that is, do they know that dead plant material eventually decays and becomes part of the soil?

The children should remember to explain what each object in their underworld symbolises. This could be used as a springboard to a reflective writing task which focuses on scene-setting and developing descriptions of place.

This activity can also be repeated in spring, especially just after Easter. However, reverse the focus and look at 'scenes of new life'.

Idea 4.20 Metasaga

Metasaga is a leadership development tool created by Kate Coutts, a head teacher on Shetland. It is about exploring the local cultural and physical landscape with the aim of assisting a person to 'reframe their thinking using metaphor, narrative, tradition and artefacts found in their own physical environment'.[2]

The approach works very well with primary-aged children. It enables children to think about themselves and reflect on their life. This involves setting up a short walk with stops at different places. The stopping places can be big features, such as a church, or less obvious objects, like a shrub or small flower. At each stop, children are asked to:

- Consider the values represented by the feature.
- Ask questions, particularly those which make a personal connection to the feature. The questions set by children are often the ones adults find most difficult to answer!

---

2 See <http://metasaga.wikispaces.com>

■ Undertake a simple task connected to the feature and the discussion. This may be writing, drawing or other ideas that have come from the children or the teacher.

■ Think about music that matches the mood of the place and to remind them of the discussion and activity there.

Greater detail on how to set up a Metasaga can be found on the website. You can also read about examples created by other teachers and contribute to the growing collection.

Reviewing activities

Reviewing sessions help children make sense of what has happened and how they feel about it. In my experience, the more opportunities children are given for reflecting on their learning in different ways, the more adept they get at expressing their thoughts.

For lots of different approaches to reviewing and reflecting, have a look at Roger Greenaway's Active Reviewing website and booklists.[3] He is a specialist who has developed reviewing methodologies that are widely used within the outdoor sector. Although not all the activities on the website are suitable for primary-aged children, many are and most work well outside – a good example is the rope review (see Idea 4.26). There are also some useful articles about the need for reviewing in an outdoor context.

Idea 4.21 Clay ball collections

Find a small, strong twig about the length of your palm and attach a piece of string to it so that it hangs down. Then take a fist-sized lump of clay and mould this into a ball around the string so that you have created a clay ball on a string.

Ask each child to find something interesting that is no longer than their index finger. Once everyone has brought their object back to the gathering circle, the clay ball can be carefully passed around and each child should stick their object into the ball. As they do so, they should add a reflective statement about the session. For example:

■ What part of the session they enjoyed the most and why.

■ Why this object is interesting and what is says about them.

■ What part of their lives the object reminds them of.

---

3 See <http://reviewing.co.uk>

Idea 4.22 Talking sticks

When gathering together at the start or end of an outdoor session, introduce a talking stick. This can be any stick found in the grounds or wood. If you can get permission to cut a special branch from a living tree, this is especially useful because additional meaning can be given to the stick in terms of the folklore and properties of the tree from which it came.

The children may only talk when they are holding the stick. This can help to create a special atmosphere – a talking stick may only be held by a person who speaks from the heart and speaks the truth. The stick should always be passed clockwise.

As the outdoor sessions continue, the stick can be replaced with a larger one to signify the growth of the group. This can happen periodically throughout the year as important milestones are reached, or when there have been friendship issues that the children have managed to sort out positively and the class dynamics have been strengthened.

The stick can also serve as a memory stick, with an object from each session attached or tied to it. This can help the children to recall previous sessions outside.

Idea 4.23 Line reviews

A simple reflective activity is to draw a line or extend a rope along the ground and number it from 0 to 10.

Ask children questions such as:

- How tricky did you find …?
- How successful were your group at …?
- How kind were you to other people in your group?

The children have to rate themselves on a scale of 0 to 10 by standing at the appropriate number on the line. Once a group or class have done this, and whilst they are still in line, talk briefly with the children about why they chose to place themselves where they did. An interesting extension can be for one child to evaluate where others have placed themselves, and if they give a good reason, moving certain individuals to a different place on the line. For example: 'Fred helped Mary stay in the hoop, so I think he was kinder than 2 out of 10. I'm moving Fred to 5.'

Idea 4.24 Human scattergraphs

Scattergraphs are useful for plotting the relationship between two variables on a graph. The results are usually scattered and a line of best fit is drawn. At the primary school level, the experience of creating a human scattergraph should be kept simple. Focus on whether a correlation can be found between two variables – for example, after completing a team challenge, ask the children to undertake a line review (see Idea 4.23) to rate how challenging they found the activity.

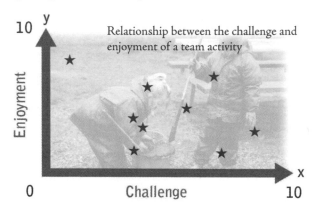
Relationship between the challenge and enjoyment of a team activity

Next, ask the children to consider how much they enjoyed the activity, on a scale of 0 to 10, only this time, the children (x) move into a scattergraph formation. See figure (right) for example.

This will allow you to gauge whether you have pitched the lesson at the appropriate level.

Idea 4.24 A sensory review

The sensory review is an interesting group review. In groups of five, each person selects one sense to feed back to the rest of the class. You may wish to have cards with a sense written on each one for handing out to each group. For example, when thinking about what was the best part of the session:

- Sight: I saw a kestrel dive out of the sky.

- Hearing: I heard Mr Walker praise our group for working well.

- Taste: I tasted the sweet success of victory because our team won.

- Smell: I smelled the flower I found.

- Touch: I felt the warm sun on my face.

Idea 4.26 Rope review

The rope review is a nice way to end a session, particularly if ropes have been used. You need a length of rope which is long enough for everyone in the class to hold on to. Tie the rope together so that it creates a circle with at least one knot in it.

The rope starts being moved clockwise through everyone's hands. A person may only speak when they feel the knot. He or she must say, 'Stop', hold the knot and speak their thoughts about the activity. The rope can then change direction or continue moving clockwise. Not everyone has to say something.

To extend this activity symbols, objects or cards can be added to the knots which direct the conversation. For example, one knot may state 'Feelings' and another may have 'The best part of this session was ...' or 'This session gave me an idea for ...' [4]

Thinking, Reflecting and Reviewing checklist

Have you:

- Looked around your grounds or outdoor space for good places for children to work alone?

- Started to initiate activities which involve children working in their own place alone?

- Begun to include reviewing and reflecting activities undertaken outside with your class?

- Considered how to feed the ideas and thoughts gained from reviewing and reflection activities into further outdoor or indoor experiences?

---

4 For further ideas related to this activity, see R. Greenaway, *Turn-Taking When Reviewing in a Group* (n.d.). Available at: <http://reviewing.co.uk/articles/turntaking.htm>

CHAPTER 5

Creating and Constructing

The act of creating something is central to the thinking process. Being able to express your thoughts and feelings, beyond the spoken or written word, offers a different way of communicating. Outdoor work can facilitate alternative forms of self-expression through the practical nature of many activities. For example, a child may prefer to create a structure, such as a bird-feeding station, as a route into studying and learning about birds and other creatures.

In this chapter we look at:

- Den building as a constructive way into curriculum work.

- Art and music activities – these enable children to express their thoughts and ideas through exploring rhythm, sound, texture, colour and form. Being outside provides a range of stimuli and a completely different working space.

Den building

Dens are valued special places, especially if they can be left *in situ* and children can use them freely during playtimes and out of school. Skills will be developed informally which teachers can capitalise on during class time.

Den building is a social activity and children will readily work with each other to create dens. Practice is needed as there are skills involved, such as tying knots and being able to attach a piece

of material to whatever structures the school grounds have to offer. Usually a lot of creativity and problem-solving happens as a natural by-product. By observing and noting down improvements in the design and construction processes, you will quickly find that a progression of skills develops.

Dens give children solitude amidst the frenzy of a packed school day. Providing den building materials in areas where children have expressed a preference for being alone can be a successful playtime or calming activity – a DIY chill-out space!

Den building taps into a basic human need for shelter and creating a home away from home. This can be adapted and extended considerably for various projects. For example, in Steiner Waldorf schools, at Key Stage 2, each class usually builds a little house as a year-long project. This transfers den-building skills into house-building ones!

Inviting a Forest School leader, Scout leader or bushcraft expert to an outdoor session to provide advice, tips and guidance on den building can be a useful way of kick-starting the process. Bear in mind, though, that they may be more used to woodlands rather than flat bare ground. Parent volunteers often enjoy den building too.

After building a den or fort, children can undertake all sorts of linked writing activities. If building a den isn't possible in your school, then nooks, crannies and other hideaways can be used instead. Link these to relevant themes such as solitude, calm, peace and so on.

Den building can involve a sophisticated design process. Set clear briefs or use recognised den designs to develop the children's practical skills. Tarpaulins are available in a huge range of sizes, colours, types and densities, although old shower curtains, sheets or other lengths of material can be used instead. By exploring how to build dens, the children can learn experientially what works best in different places, seasons and weather.

Idea 5.1 How to build the perfect den

The art of building a den relies on being able to make the most of an outdoor space and using any available materials creatively. Ask the children in your class for their thoughts about the perfect den and to create a list of criteria prior to a practical den-building activity.

Afterwards, the children can reflect on their experiences and how easy it was to build a really good den. What tips and advice would they now give about den building? Compile a class book of advice and written instructions, or make your own films about how to build dens. Include tips such as how to find or make seats, ways of creating a comfy bed to lie on and so on.

Idea 5.2 Create real estate

In this activity, children begin by looking at how estate agents advertise homes both online and in brochures – they should pick out the key features and terminology. For example, they may notice that a good view and a garage add value to a property. Once they have an idea of what estate agents are looking for, the children have to design and build their own 'real estate' dens. They can then give guided tours of their properties and decide on their monetary value (probably priceless!). They could also discuss selling tactics – for example, what smells will entice a person to make an offer for

their property? What features are especially attractive? Finally, the children need to photograph their den and create a schedule for their newly built property.

Idea 5.3 Investigate the science of den building

Does the construction of a den affect its ability to protect its inhabitants from the rain? What if the same building materials are used in every design? Ask the children to design a fair test to find out, and write a scientific report based on the results of their findings.

Idea 5.4 Get tied in knots

Show your class how to make different knots and where to access this information – for example, there are some great knots apps for tablets and smartphones. Knots provide a practical reason for following instructions and directions. Have small lengths of rope available for children to practise their knot work and to demonstrate their ability. Perhaps hold knot-tying competitions.

Idea 5.5 Den-building homework

Set homework tasks which involve researching different shelters or creating ones in a different outdoor space, such as a backyard or garden. Is this easier or harder than in the school grounds? Encourage children to take photos and share their findings. If children put 'how to build a den' into a YouTube search, a good choice of videos will come up which will give them more ideas. However, do remind children to consider the safety and environmental aspects of some types of den making – for example, some natural dens involve cutting down branches.

Idea 5.6 Learn traditional building skills

Invite traditional craftspeople to show the class their skills – for example, they could learn how to thatch a roof, build a dry-stone wall or construct a cob oven. The children could also research local building techniques. These can be used to extend and develop their den-building skills and link their efforts to real-world equivalents. This can be a useful way into improving the school grounds. Local community colleges sometimes run building courses. They will have students who need to undertake practical projects who may be prepared to help.

Idea 5.7 Old tent day

Organise a tent day where everyone brings their old tents to school. Which designs are the easiest to erect? Which instruction leaflets are the easiest to follow and why? Which work best for hanging out or working in? The children could review the designs in the language and format of the gear reviews in outdoor magazines.

Idea 5.8 3D shape structures

Making 3D nets and structures is surprisingly tricky. It works best if children have practised using square lashings and other ways of attaching sticks together. Which group can make the biggest den with just twelve one-metre sticks or bamboo canes?

Idea 5.9 Design animal shelters

Children also enjoy designing houses for mammals, birds or insects. Wildlife organisations often sell a variety of animal homes and bird boxes, so looking at their websites for ideas can be helpful. Some are definitely works of art and this can inspire some very creative results. It is worth discussing whether animals prefer function over gimmicky design features, and children will need to consider carefully the needs of each animal species. For example, tawny owls need a very different sort of nesting box to blue tits. Where such homes are sited matters too. Ensure the children find the most suitable location for their creations, which meets the requirements of the animal for which it was designed.

Idea 5.10 A global dimension to den building

The aim of this activity is for older children to experience the inequality of the current trading systems that operate in our world and to help them understand about issues such as giving aid and countries supporting each other.

Split the class into den-building groups of around five or six children. First, give the groups a competitive activity so that the groups are ranked first, second and so on – for example, have a quick team quiz with five short answers.

Next, explain that each group has to create a den that is big enough for their group to live in comfortably. There needs to be standing room as well as sitting room, and the shelter should be waterproof.

Then hand out the materials. The team with the top score gets the best den-building materials. The group should be given lots of lovely items such as: comfy seats, drinks and snacks, sleeping bags, music to play and plenty of den-building material such as Velcro, ropes, string, pegs, sheets, tarpaulins, netting, shower curtains and so on.

The next best team gets quite a lot of resources but without the luxury items – drinks, snacks, music, seating or sleeping bags.

The next team (or two) gets no luxury items and a basic sheet or tarpaulin with one item of attachment – maybe the pegs or just the string.

The team that performed the worst gets a box and nothing else.

Give the teams a time limit for building their shelters and state any ground rules that you think are needed. Then stand back and let them get on with the task. Observe what happens. Do not offer advice or suggestions unless some mediation between groups is needed. Even then, try to let the groups work out what to do and make their own decisions.

At the end of the activity, let each group show off their dens. Then discuss the following issues:

- What happened? Ask children to describe their experience.

- What were positive aspects of the experience? Which groups managed to successfully build their den and why? What other positive situations came out of the activity?

- What were negative aspects? How did children or groups work through these?

- How did the children feel at the start, middle and end of the activity? How did they try to manage these feelings?

- If the activity was repeated, what would the children change about the experience?

- How does this activity link to how countries behave towards each other in terms of resources?

The activity is very experiential in its approach. It is a powerful mechanism for helping children to understand how human behaviour at a local level can influence international decisions and actions. They learn experientially to trade and barter, although it is not uncommon for some groups simply not to share, or to hand over only or two items. What is important is that the class manage this situation and the adults let the children work things out. Only intervene if really necessary.

Expressing thoughts and ideas through music

The outdoors provides children with different sensory experiences and stimuli which mean there are new ways for them to explore and create music. Ask a music teacher to show you and your class how to check the acoustics of different parts of your outdoor space so that you can make the most of each area.

Many musical instruments are robust and portable. In countries all over the world, people listen to and play music outside. Think of the growth of music festivals in recent decades and how these events celebrate music in a range of outdoor settings.

Singing takes place everywhere and helps children make connections between their body, sounds and the environment.

Idea 5.11 Sing songs in different places

Sing songs whilst you move from one place to another and as a way of passing time on a journey. After all, marching songs work well when everyone is marching along! They can also be sung to mark the transition between activities or as an aural signal that a job is coming to an end.

Sing songs in different parts of the grounds. Which songs sound best where? Does the mood of a song best suit an atmosphere that comes out of a place? If you sing the same song in different places, where does it sound best?

Idea 5.12 Every breath you take

What is the furthest distance a person can walk whilst singing a well-known song or nursery rhyme? Can the children design a fair test to find this out?

Idea 5.13 Use songs and music as a stimulus for outdoor activities

There are many songs and well-known pieces of music with themes which lend themselves to outdoor activities, so try to introduce some variety. It is worth creating your own outdoor playlist as this will save you time searching for tracks for future lessons.

One teaching friend got her class to listen to and read the lyrics of 'Moanin' Lisa Blues' from the album *The Simpsons Sing the Blues*. They used the format of the song to look for problems and things they wanted to moan about in the school grounds – they also came up with solutions. The class developed a blues song about their grounds which they sang to the original soundtrack.

Idea 5.14 An outdoor music wall

Music walls can be made anywhere. It is a great way of recycling different materials and old instruments. Ask your class to look online at the range of outdoor music walls and use these to brainstorm ideas for constructing one of their own. They should think about:

- What materials can be acquired for free?

- Where would be the best place to site the music wall?

- Does the music wall need to be portable or can it be left outside? How will it be maintained and who is responsible for doing this?

- Who can provide advice? Does anyone know any musicians or practical people, such as joiners?

- Is permission needed to undertake this project?

Idea 5.15 Create musical instruments outdoors

The making of musical instruments can become an ongoing technology project as children research, experiment and modify their work. With older children, encourage them to move beyond apparatus that sounds clunky into more finely tuned instruments. This works best if you focus on one musical aspect, such as developing and exploring rhythms. Here are some suggestions:

- Collect gravel, seeds or other natural materials to put inside tubs, toilet tubes, etc.

- Test out the pitch, tone and sounds of fences, walls and other features.

- Older children can experiment with tone and scale, such as water in glass jars or using different spanners and types/lengths of wood as sticks. They can also look at more complex rhythms and the mixing of sounds.

- Have a look at the Child's Play Music website[1] for lots more ideas and links to video clips. Alternatively, check out the video by Landfill Harmonic on YouTube.[2] Their instruments have all been made from recycled objects and this can add an interesting global dimension for older classes.

---

1 See <http://childsplaymusic.com.au>
2 See <http://www.youtube.com/watch?v=fXynrsrTKbI>

Expressing thoughts and ideas through art

Perhaps the biggest challenge when undertaking art activities outside is to narrow down the possibilities. There are several reasons for this:

- The weather and seasons make for variety and a natural stimulus for artwork.

- Inspirational public art can be found in many places beyond art galleries and museums. For example, take a look at the work of Antony Gormley, Charles Jencks and Gordon Young.

- Many people undertake a variety of art activities as hobbies. Ask your children's parents and see if any are up for supporting a series of art sessions outside.

- Professional artists quite often work outside and can be hired to work with classes on specific features or projects.

- The work of lots of famous artists depicts outdoor scenes. The Canadian Group of Seven are renowned for their wilderness landscapes.[3] Many impressionist paintings are creative interpretations of continental scenes. In the UK, there is a long and varied tradition of outdoor art from artists such as Gainsborough, Constable and Turner. Apply the ideas of these and other artists to outdoor activities.

Idea 5.16 Art investigations outside

Encourage children to ask questions and devise ways of exploring the outdoor environment. Here are some ideas to get you started:

- Do straight lines exist in nature?

- Is it possible to find all the colours of the rainbow in nature, except in a rainbow?

- Why would texture matter to a cyclist or skateboarder?

- Does colour make the world a happier or a more sad place?

- Is it possible for an artist to lose his or her sense of perspective?

Idea 5.17 Make the most of the elements

There are seven key visual elements: line, shape, form, colour, tone, pattern and texture. These can be explored outside. Generally, combining two elements at a time works well – for example, encouraging children to experiment with colour and tone, or pattern and texture. This is

---

3 See <http://groupofsevenart.com>

particularly helpful when exploring land artists, such as Andy Goldsworthy, Chris Drury, Richard Long, Marc Pouyet, Richard Shilling and others.

When asking children to evaluate artwork or look at the work of others, use these seven visual elements. For example, one group can discuss and feed back their thoughts about the patterns observed, another group could look at how texture has been used and so on.

Idea 5.18 Outdoor doodles

Art requires lots of practice to obtain mastery, so encourage children to doodle outdoors. This can be a useful activity for children who complete other assignments early. Give them specific tasks to develop this habit, such as:

- Stick a found object, such as a leaf, onto a piece of card and turn it into a picture by adding more detail onto and around it.

- Copy patterns found outside but insert them into different objects (e.g. draw a leaf but make the veins look like a chicken wire boundary fence, draw a wall but replace the bricks with a repeating flower design).

- Doodle with smells – collect odours on a piece of card and present them in interesting outlines. It's the DIY version of scratch 'n' sniff cards! Sandpaper is particularly useful for this activity.

- Draw or create objects within objects, just like Russian dolls. How many sticks within sticks is it possible to construct?

- Experiment with plants and other materials as drawing mediums or dyes. This can work especially well on calico. If the cotton is cut into triangles, then you can quickly make some bunting out of the work to be hung inside or out.

Idea 5.19 The never-ending line

If your class were to draw a line outside, or create one from found materials, what would it look like and where would it go? How would they manage the teamwork involved to undertake the task? One person must always be actually creating the line at the point where it is moving. Think about whether the line can be permanent or whether it will need to be tidied away afterwards. Get the class to experiment individually on a piece of paper beforehand to help them understand the challenges involved in completing the task on a larger scale. The children may find it easier to work in small groups rather than as a whole class.

Idea 5.20 Dream your school building

Painting is to dream. When the dream is over, I don't remember anything I dreamed about. The painting, however, remains. It is the harvest of my dream.

Friedensreich Hundertwasser

Hundertwasser was famed for his dynamic, colourful artwork and beautiful buildings, which often have no straight lines and include trees growing out of them and vegetation on the roof-tops. He was an outspoken environmentalist and one of the earliest proponents of guerrilla gardening (see Idea 9.20).

After studying paintings and photos by Hundertwasser, take the children outside to sketch the school building. However, they should add to their drawings aspects which could make the building more fun, unique and colourful, as well as practical or environmentally friendly features. Sometimes a step-by-step approach is easier – for example, they could focus on specific aspects of the building design, such as windows and doors, then add in the colour and detail afterwards.

Idea 5.21 Undertake a public art investigation

What public art exists and where can it be found within walking distance from your school? Remember, some works may be housed in libraries, churches, museums and other places as well as outside. Set up a class survey, which will include a way of rating the artwork you find, according to whatever criteria the children decide matter to them. Take photos and create a presentation. Send your findings to the arts development officer or cultural coordinator at your local authority, your local councillor or even the local press and see what response your class receives.

Idea 5.22 Hidden acts of art

If there is little or no public art to be found in your locality, then the children could find and record and photograph 'hidden' acts of art. This might be:

- A stained glass window above a door.

- A beautifully designed garden.

- A hairdresser's shop that creates innovative hair designs.

- A decorative pattern of bird droppings.

- Whatever your children think adds interest and creativity to the world.

They can then use their records and photographs to create an exhibition.

Idea 5.23 Outdoor art whatever the weather

Make the most of the weather and seasons for the variety they bring to art outdoors:

- Google 'snow sculptures' and use these images to inspire the children to create forms beyond the traditional snowman.

- Collect together paint, food colouring, squeezy bottles, syringes, pipes and other bits and pieces for creating colourful artwork in the snow.

- Ask the children to create a picture using watercolour paints or draw on card with felt-tip pens outside in the rain. How can the rain be used to add to the effect of a picture?

- Create shadow art on sunny days. Ask the class to think of ways of capturing their shadowy creations.

Creating and Constructing checklist

Have you:

- Raided your art cupboard for the oldest and most unwanted resources? Do the same with the musical instruments. Have a sort out and remove any broken items. Brainstorm ideas for their use outside with your class.

- Spent some time searching the Internet for outdoor art and music ideas?

- Put together a den-building kit? If you are short of funds, ask parents and the school janitor for unwanted items. Pound shops often have various camping items, especially during the summer months, and supermarkets usually have sales of outdoor gear in August or September.

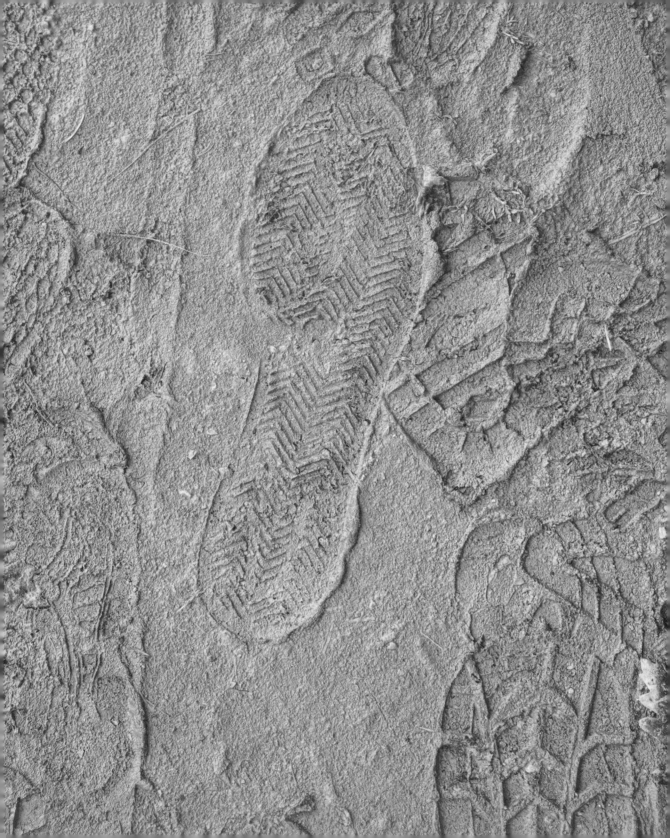

CHAPTER 6

A Sense of Adventure

Think about adventures you had in your childhood. What made an activity or experience adventurous? When you ask children or adults these questions, you receive a range of responses, such as:

- There needs to be an element of the unknown and of discovery.

- Risk and excitement.

- Obstacles to overcome.

- Something unexpected happening in an ordinary situation, like walking down the street.

- Experiencing for real or recreating adventures read about in books such as Mark Twain's *The Adventures of Tom Sawyer*, Enid Blyton's Famous Five series or Arthur Ransome's *Swallows and Amazons*.

- Doing things that aren't allowed.

- There is a story surrounding it in some way or a narrative is created.

- It is about doing things independently, either with friends or alone.

When considering adventure and incorporating this into education provision, taking children to an indoor climbing wall may not necessarily cut it in terms of their expectations and understanding of adventure.

The dictionary definition of adventure is an 'unusual and exciting, typically hazardous, experience or activity'. Judging by the comments above, it seems that adventure appears to be mainly created by the participants themselves and is not always found in organised adventurous activities, such as a high ropes course.

Given that most teachers are not qualified to teach adventurous activities, such as rock climbing or sailing, the challenge is to create anticipation and a sense of adventure. This allows us to be innovative when it comes to including an adventurous element in our lessons. The children, and sometimes the teacher, may not know what is going to happen when you start out.

I believe that children's perceptions of adventure are age related or follow some form of developmental progression. For little children, discovering 'treasures' by digging in a mud patch can represent a great adventure. Children who are a little older see mystery and detective work as key parts of adventure. Exploring the local area by themselves is often cited as an adventure by ten- to twelve-year-olds. One Czech friend described his teenage adventures sleeping out in woodland close to his home and wondering if the nearby noises were wild boars!

Thus, the starting point is to find out what the children in your class consider to be an adventure and what will hold their interest. From this point, you can make learning into an exciting adventure. Remember, however, that one child's idea of an adventure may be very different to another. Often as not, adventure is a frame of mind and an emotional as much as a physical experience.

Idea 6.1 Present activities in the spirit of an adventure

How we present outdoor activities to children can make the difference between what they perceive to be a mundane activity and one which ignites their interest and curiosity. David Sobel, a well-respected place-based educator, observes: 'If I suggested to my children that we were going on a walk, they complained. However, if I opened with "Let's go on an adventure," they were much more recruitable.' [1]

Also look for opportunities to include surprises and unexpected twists and turns in a series of events. Very often, the interruptions and unexpected happenings that occur outside can be used spontaneously for mini adventures.

Idea 6.2 Give children time to reflect on an adventurous experience

Giving children reflection time allows the story of the adventure to be consolidated and shared, and for the children involved to add their own thoughts and feelings. This can enhance the memory and sense of adventure. Use prompts such as:

- What happened?
- What were the highs and lows of the experience?
- How did you feel about the experience overall?
- Is there anything you would change or do differently next time?
- What have you learned from the experience?

---

1 D. Sobel, *Childhood and Nature: Design Principles for Education* (Portland, OR: Stenhouse Publishers, 2008), p. 21.

Rather than record this in written form, encourage the children to use materials in the environment to illustrate their reflections. For example, a stick might be used as a person and be walked along a wall to explain a dilemma within the adventure. This makes a good alternative to having to undertake a write-up.

Idea 6.3 Retell events in an adventurous way

Think about a time you have sat next to a friend telling you about a mundane event but who managed to make it into the most amazing adventurous experience. Audacious accounts can be a lot of fun – it is a way of making an everyday event more exciting. Encourage children to use storytelling techniques, such as:

- The power of gesture.
- Use outdoor features as elements of the story – for example, a nearby tree may represent a house, or a patch of mud the nearby pond.
- Sudden changes of storyline.
- Use of different sounds.

- Lots of movement and a mixture of large/small motor movements.

- Active silence through gesture and facial expression.

- Eye contact with the audience.

- Focus upon the language of adventure. What words and phrases can be used which promote adventure?

- Your positioning and movement around the group/outdoor setting.

This can happen orally outside at a gathering circle or can be completed after an exciting day out. Real adventures will produce real writing from children during and after the event. Depending on their age, a structure for this may need to be supplied with a series of prompts. It is also worth hiring a professional storyteller to work with your class on developing their oral storytelling skills.

Idea 6.4 Undertake drama activities

Drama happens naturally outside and can be used to make the most ordinary situation extraordinary. There are several ways to consider the role of drama. It can be taught through:

- A drama-based enquiry approach, such as Mantle of the Expert.[2]

- The use of drama games and activities in different curriculum areas.

- The teaching of specific drama skills in an outdoor context (e.g. mime, performance skills).

- Provision of props where the outdoor environment is used as a stimulus.

This provides opportunities for learning other skills in context. For example, you could develop writing roles for different characters, such as a detective or journalist, who may need to write down notes. Try to have simple props available, like mini writing kits (see Idea 6.5) or an outdoor dressing-up box (see Idea 9.17).

Idea 6.5 Create mini writing kits for mini adventures

Have mini mobile writing kits ready for adventures and activities outside. Collect good stashes of the resources listed below and make them easily available for taking outside. Encourage children to experiment and think what would be useful when they are out and about, so that the items vary in line with the children's ideas and interests. For example:

- Different sorts of codes (e.g. Morse, number, runes, hieroglyphs) – this gives children ideas for inventing their own.

2 See <http://www.mantleoftheexpert.com>

- Pocket-sized pencils and notepads – always have spare, sharpened pencils.

- Rolled-up strips of paper for writing on – these can be stored in your pockets or down your sock.

- A small magnifying glass or Fresnel lens.

- Scratch sticks for leaving secret messages on leaves, etc. – cocktail sticks or used matchsticks work well for this purpose.

- Lollipop sticks for writing short messages on which can be stuck in the ground.

- Old CDs and cheap mirrors – you can write on these with dry-wipe pens.

- Sticky notes.

- Scrap card – cut up cereal boxes into small and big squares. Use crayons or permanent marker pens to write with.

- Toilet tubes – these can be stapled at either end to contain treasures and messages. They can also be coloured or decorated so they camouflage with the surroundings.

- Double-sided sticky tape – this works well for sticking found items onto paper or card.

- A5 and A3 clipboards – these tend to be more useful than the traditional A4 size.

■ Transparent tarpaulin – this makes a massive writing surface which is great for graffiti, leaving messages for others to read and general doodles. It's also good for shelter outside.

These kits can work well for free-play situations as well as formal writing activities outside. Expect rough notes and doodles – this is real writing in a more unpredictable context. Neat work is not necessary! Check whether children would like to be able to access these resources at playtime and ask them to set up workable systems for doing so. (Note: this will involve some trial and error. If your school is short of funds then ask for donations of items such as sticky notes, empty cereal boxes, etc. from parents and the local community.)

Idea 6.6 Adventure spots

School grounds and local areas may not seem like the setting for adventures to happen – so many are flat squares of asphalt and playing field. But sometimes everything is not as it seems! To make a place more adventurous does not necessarily require a high ropes course, a rapid river and a jungle setting. After all, Alice went down a rabbit hole to have her adventure in Wonderland …

Get your children to find, mark on a map and photograph all the 'adventurous' places which might exist in a seemingly normal playground. This might include:

- The dangerous parts of the playground.
- Locked doors.
- Forbidden areas or places that are out-of-bounds.
- Scary places.
- Little-known or seldom-visited places within the school or school grounds.
- Holes of different sorts.
- Tunnels and archways.
- Dens, nooks and crannies.
- Places that are full of surprise, the unknown or the unexpected.

This can lead on to similar discussions about the local area and what adventures the children have had there. Be prepared for some surprises – and for exploring some of these places with your class. Remember that these places can be springboards for learning adventures inside too.

Idea 6.7 Use props to make quick changes to an area outside

Props that can be deployed to transform an area include:

- Shells and other treasure which can be hidden in gravel to be spontaneously discovered.
- Biodegradable, real-flower confetti can be sprinkled to create a faint fairy trail.
- Use coffee beans as a sensory mulch in planters – smells stimulate memories and thoughts.
- Signs or little messages left around the school for children to find.
- Curtains at the end of a willow tunnel or archway – when the children go through them an adventure begins …

Idea 6.8 Make your school grounds more physically adventurous

There is an increasing body of research which suggests that natural play spaces – which include trees, willow structures, dens, a range of surfaces, different changes in height and levels upon which to play – benefit children's cooperative, social and physical skills. Open-ended materials, often referred to as 'loose parts', can also be made available for children to use in these spaces and aid creative and imaginative play. These include wooden discs, sticks, guttering, tyres, tarpaulins and carefully thought out access to water.

In the medium to long term, look at improving your school grounds to create a child-friendly adventurous playspace. A good first step would be to contact Learning through Landscapes[3] or any other school ground charity that advocates a participative approach. Their professional advisers have lots of ideas and suggestions which truly involve children in the whole process from start to finish. This is another adventure in itself! It is also worth seeing if there is a local adventure playground which you can visit with your class so that the children have a better understanding of the possibilities.

Idea 6.9 Keep the end open

There is nothing like a bit of mystery and the sense of the unknown. As a child, I used to hate the afternoon walks my mum insisted we took, but I was always up for a 'penny walk'. This is where you flip a coin every time you reach a road junction: heads means you turn right, tails means you go left. We never knew where we would end up and we would have a lot of fun guessing!

A similar activity involves 'following your nose'. When walking with a group, you may not have a set destination but simply decide by consensus or otherwise which path to take.

Both these activities can be followed up back inside by challenging children to see if they can accurately retrace the journey using Google Earth's ruler tool.

---

3 See <http://www.ltl.org.uk>

Idea 6.10 Gently stretch children out of their comfort zone

Coaxing children out of their comfort zone can be done in several ways. Just spending a whole day outside can be a new challenge for some of them. Always remember to build in opportunities for the children to review and reflect on these experiences, as this is an important part of the 'stretching' process.

If your class is going to a residential centre or is spending the day undertaking outdoor pursuits, then start with some linked preparatory activities. For example, prior to visiting a cave or going caving, try:

- Setting up a trail to be completed blindfolded or with their eyes closed.

- Sensory activities which involve using other senses apart from sight (e.g. blind man's bluff).

- Watching a sunset, followed by twilight and nighttime arriving. Hold a Dark Sky Party and watch the stars come out.[4] There are useful apps available for digital devices which can help you identify the constellations.

Idea 6.11 Link adventurous activities to other subjects

Explore opportunities for adventurous activities for your class and then use these to develop other skills back at school. For example, physics in action can be seen in the following activities:

- Canoeing links nicely to developing children's concepts of buoyancy, floating and sinking, and energy transfer.

- Rock climbing is an ideal springboard into examining the principles behind how levers and pulleys work.

- Skiing is about friction and using gravity.

Do remember that the activities must be led by a suitably qualified instructor. Check your local authority's adventurous activities policy and guidelines for school visits.

Idea 6.12 Use an augmented reality app

Augmented reality apps add a digital layer of information – such as a global positioning system (GPS), sound or imagery – to any place when viewed via a smartphone or tablet. They come in

4 See <http://www.darkskydiscovery.org.uk>

various guises which enable children to interact with their environment in digital ways. For many younger children, this is an adventure in itself.

Apps such as Aurasma allow fantasy characters to be integrated into an outdoor space. When a device is moved over a recognisable object, a character appears on the screen. The digital content complements the real world. A good use for these types of apps is to help children explore a new space.

Older classes can design a simple treasure hunt for younger classes based upon the children locating different characters in different places (e.g. in a tree, down a hole, on a hanging basket).

Idea 6.13 Create a mission

In 2010, the Geography Collective published a little book called *Mission: Explore*, which was followed up with an iPhone app, several more books and a website.[5] This fresh approach to exploration has changed how many people see their 'mundane' local area. It fulfils the niche need for micro adventures. You may not feel every mission they suggest is suitable for your school but that

---

5 See Geography Collective, *Mission: Explore* (London: Can of Worms Kids Press, 2010) and <http://www.missionexplore.net>

is part of the attraction. Your class can use the ideas and approach to create their own missions as well as complete some of those on the website.

A Sense of Adventure checklist

Have you:

- ■ Reflected on your time as a teacher and identified what experiences you feel children found adventurous at different ages? Make a note of these to ensure you pitch your language and the way in which you facilitate an experience at the appropriate level.

- ■ Considered what you can do to create a sense of adventure when planning outdoor experiences?

- ■ Thought about how you can encourage children to develop their own adventures? Consider props and resources which you can have available to use outside to facilitate this.

- ■ Looked at traditional adventurous activities and considered how they can be woven into a topic? It is worth liaising with outdoor education providers to see if their sessions can be adjusted to ensure this happens rather than have isolated one-off experiences.

CHAPTER 7

Exploring What's Out There

This chapter is about exploring the school grounds and local area. Children enjoy hunts, trails and using maps as ways of learning. These can be devised for many projects or disciplines outside.

Trails and hunts usually take a long time to create, so bear this in mind before embarking on an idea. As much as possible, get the class to create and design trails for themselves, or for other classes to complete. This avoids the frustration of spending three hours preparing an activity after school only for it to be completed in ten minutes the next day.

For short, sharp trail activities, go miniature. This works well in featureless places because the children's imaginations get to work. For example, a small puddle can be the size of a lake to a worm trying to find its way back home.

Be mindful of the purpose of any trail, hunt or mapping activity. Possible reasons to use these include:

- As a way of assessing the children's levels of understanding and knowledge acquisition during a project.

- To develop specific mapping skills.

- To contribute to a community project (e.g. an interpretive trail around a town).

Remember to think about what happens at the end of a trail or hunt. Do the children need an exciting finale? What happens when a group or child has finished the hunt? Be prepared for groups of children finishing at different times and the levels of supervision that may be required. Look at the range of finishing tasks in Chapter 10 for some ideas or build a finishing task into the hunt or trail itself.

Idea 7.1 What do explorers need?

It can be interesting to find out what your children think an explorer is and what they do. Brainstorm this idea with your class.

- What equipment might an explorer need?

- What skills and attributes does an explorer need? For instance, how important is common sense? A gut feeling? A sixth sense?

- What sort of tasks do explorers undertake?

- Look at famous explorers, both modern and historical, and put together a list of qualities that explorers have.

Idea 7.2 Investigate disappearing trails

In the story of Hansel and Gretel, the breadcrumbs were eaten by birds. What disappearing trails could the children create? For example, creating a trail of water on a hot day. After they have come up with some ideas, get them to discuss:

- The benefits as well as the limitations of disappearing trails.

- When a disappearing might trail be needed.

- How a trail disappears.

Idea 7.3 Physical fitness trails

If children have done circuit training indoors, then they can easily adapt the idea to create a fitness trail outside. Quick ones can be created with PE equipment and children moving around a series of stations and spending an agreed amount of time at each. This works well in a small space such as a basketball court.

Alternatively, trails can be created using outdoor features. Challenge the children to come up with exercises and physical challenges that make the most of the school grounds. For example:

- Running up and down steps.

- Push-ups against a wall.

- Jumping over logs.

- Leapfrogging over low posts.

This can be a good introduction to Parkour. This is a non-competitive sport which involves seeing the potential in any environment and moving in, around and through it. There are a growing number of online Parkour games, so your class might enjoy the challenge of a real-life version.

Idea 7.4 Historical hunts

History projects can provide a useful context for children to learn the skill of setting up a trail in the school grounds. Challenge groups of children to create a series of questions and to research their answers in advance. This can be a useful assessment of their knowledge and understanding of a topic.

Next, each answer should be written on a separate piece of card and securely placed somewhere in the school grounds. The group marks the location of each answer on a map of the grounds.

Once each group has set up their own trail, they embark on a different group's trail. They will need the list of questions, so that they know which answers to look for, and the map which indicates their location. Afterwards, discuss the effectiveness of the trails and the accuracy of the maps. How would the groups increase or decrease the level of challenge?

Idea 7.5 Geocaching

Geocaching is a world-wide treasure hunting game which uses GPS.[1] In order to play, you sign up to the free website to find out where the nearest geocache is to your school. Then, using GPS or a smartphone, you enter a specific set of coordinates and attempt to find the geocache (container) hidden at that location. These may be hidden or disguised in some way. Inside the cache you will find a logbook to sign and sometimes they contain messages or presents – you remove one and replace it with another.

It is quite straightforward to set up private geocaches within your school grounds – it could be an interesting project for the children to do this for another class to complete.

Idea 7.6 Digital trails

Mobile devices, such as tablets and smartphones, provide lots of opportunities for developing hunts and trails. Ask on social media platforms such as Twitter for ideas and advice. Common examples include:

- Photo trails. These involve taking photos at different places for others to find and match. This can be undertaken as a problem-solving challenge where children have to find the correct location and take a photo from the same angle. It can be a good way to introduce photography skills, such as how to frame a photo, how to avoid a fuzzy shot, etc.

- Quick Response (QR) codes are a form of bar code that capture different forms of information, such as websites, text or photos. Each child or group will need a mobile device with a QR reader.

- Use an augmented reality app (see Idea 6.12).

Idea 7.7 Musical sticks

Take a stick on a musical walk! The children can bang the stick against various objects and surfaces to make different sounds as they walk along. How many different sounds is it possible to make with a stick? Is there anything children need to remember when undertaking this activity, regarding the use of sticks and their interactions with the environment and others?

---

1 See <http://www.geocaching.com>

Idea 7.8 Make signs, clues and directions from nature

By their nature, natural trails tend to be well camouflaged. They can be created from various materials, such as long grass tied into knots, mini stone stacks or arrows made from sticks. Your class can experiment beforehand and come up with their own designs. It is a good idea to discuss the pros and cons of the markers. For example:

- Length of time needed to make each marker.

- How well they blend into the landscape and whether this matters or not.

- The purpose of the trail. Is it to practise way-finding? Is it to guide people to look at specific features?

- Is the trail temporary or permanent?

If your school is in a very urban environment, brainstorm with your class for alternative environmental clues which could be used.

- Could eco-friendly white paint be used to create fake bird droppings?

- What about gravel or small stones?

- Can paper be rolled up and stuck in certain places, such as under stones or in cracks in the walls?

Idea 7.9 Songline your space

Songlines are a very effective form of pathway which some indigenous Australian peoples use for route finding. The songlines are recorded not by maps in the usual sense but through traditional songs, dances, stories and paintings. Those who know the songlines are able to navigate across the land by repeating the words or movements, which describe the location of key landmarks.

It can be very interesting to give and follow directions using songs and stories. In groups, children could devise a songline to guide other groups on a route around part of an outdoor space. The children will need to consider:

- The key features within the school grounds and what these might represent.

- Interesting markings or patterns in the environment which might be useful way markers.

- A known tune to which words can be added. Decide whether the words need to rhyme – although this does make the task harder.

- How to teach another group the songline. This means that, initially, the directions may need to be given for moving across a small space where one group can hear another group singing the song.

Afterwards, discuss the effectiveness of this approach. Is it easier to remember instructions that are sung or written down? What are the advantages and disadvantages of both methods? How does singing instructions impact on how a feature is viewed?

Idea 7.10 Introduce scavenger hunts

Scavenger hunts involve finding objects in the surrounding area. Usually they are collected and shown to the adult leaders before being returned to their original positions. There are some factors to think about when planning a scavenger hunt with your class:

- Make the activity purposeful. Think about why a scavenger hunt is needed. Is it an alternative to 'find something interesting' outlined in Chapter 3?

- Be subject- or project-specific. If necessary, this could be a form of assessment of knowledge or understanding. (See also the maths scavenger hunt in Idea 7.12.)

■ Prepare group scavenger hunts as finishing-off activities. Write each challenge on a piece of card and have them laid out on the ground. Children place their found objects beside each card and everyone helps to complete the scavenger hunt.

■ Remember to use all the senses, if possible. Think about texture, size, shape and other properties of the objects the children should collect.

■ If collecting opposites, then use egg boxes or paint palettes so that matching items can be placed opposite each other. For example, you may challenge children to find three rough and three smooth objects as a starter activity for looking at textures in art.

■ Cameras can be used to take photos of different items. This works well if objects are too big to be moved. Remind the children to stick to the order on their list for ease of checking.

■ Challenge children to make up their own scavenger hunts. This is also a good assessment of their understanding of a concept. Encourage them to think about what makes a really good scavenger hunt and why.

■ Remember that items should be returned to where they belong, unless they are needed for an indoor follow-up activity.

Idea 7.11 Differentiate scavenger hunt activities

Scavenger hunt is a generic term and differentiation is needed for different age ranges. Very young children usually start with objects. As children get older, they can move onto photos or symbols and then words and phrases. Here is an example of how to make a scavenger hunt increasingly more challenging:

■ Show the class one object. The children have to go and find the same object and bring it back to the gathering circle. Progress to two, then three objects to be found at the same time.

■ Show the class a basket of objects. The children have to find the same objects, put them in their own basket and return to the gathering circle to check they have located all the objects.

■ Children work in pairs. Each pair is told what object to find and bring back to the teacher. They show the teacher their object and receive the next challenge.

■ Children work in pairs. Each pair is given a slip of paper with a set of photos or illustrations of the objects to be found.

■ Give the children close-up photos of objects or showing just part of an object (e.g. one petal of a daisy, half a beech leaf). The children have to work out what it is and then locate the objects.

- Give the children anagrams which need to be unscrambled in order to work out what objects they have to find (e.g. norca = acorn).

Idea 7.12 Mathematical scavenger hunts

Rather than collecting objects for the sake of it, incorporate a mathematical element to reinforce key maths ideas covered recently in class. For example, for a measurement hunt, the children could be asked to find:

- A twig exactly 20 cm long.
- Three pebbles measuring a total of 250 mm when laid in a row.
- Two trees spaced more than 4 metres apart.
- A way of measuring your height without using a measuring stick, tape or other standard unit.
- Something which can be put together to make 1 metre.
- Something that can be squashed to less than 10 cm.
- Something which can't be measured in terms of its length, width or height.
- Something which grows when being measured.

These ideas can be extended to shape number hunts, angle hunts, symmetry discoveries and so on.

Idea 7.13 Develop mapping skills

Acquire a variety of maps of the local area and school grounds for children to use. This can include street maps, historical maps, Ordinance Survey maps in different scales, print-outs of Google maps, Bing maps and other digital maps, such as satellite maps.

Make sure the children develop their geographical knowledge and learn the basics, such as what makes a map a map, the use of symbols, scale, position and orientation of maps. Having class-sized maps (see Idea 7.15) of the world and the UK painted on the playground can be handy for locating cities and geographical features.

Idea 7.14 Make a map of the school grounds

Mapping the school grounds works well if there is a hill or vantage point that children can use. Give out A3 clipboards and let the children walk around the grounds, sketching, taking photos and building up the information that will enable them to create a map. Using Google Earth may also help. Their maps can then be photocopied or used for other tasks. This adds value to the maps and an incentive to make them accurate and readable.

Idea 7.15 Model map making outside

To make a class-sized world map, the children should stand in a circle and a chalk circle is drawn around them. The children should then look at a map of the world and work out where the continents should be drawn within their circle.

The children themselves can represent different features on the map by standing where a country or city is located or by annotating the map with natural materials (e.g. cities are stones, prairies are grass clippings, rainforest is made up of leaves). The children can be asked to stand on different parts of the map as a way of developing their knowledge.

Idea 7.16 Go orienteering

Orienteering provides a sporting application of map work that develops navigation skills. It is great fun combining the need to be physically fit with practical problem-solving. It is possible to get orienteering maps created of your school grounds for a fee. There are also fixed orienteering courses in many local parks, woodlands and country estates. Contact British Orienteering for more information.[2]

Idea 7.17 Multisensory maps and trails

If maps are visual representations of the world, then how can your class create multisensory maps or trails which rely on sound, textures, smells and even tastes? This can lead to a number of different activities, such as:

- Blindfold trails – children can create rope trails to be undertaken blindfolded.
- Sound maps (see Idea 4.9).
- How can children add texture to a plain piece of ground that will make an interesting barefoot walk?

---

2 See <http://www.britishorienteering.org.uk>

Idea 7.18 Create 'Who dunnit?' games

Who dunnit? games are usually literacy-based problem-solvers. For example, challenge your class to adapt a game of Cluedo to your outdoor space. Identify places in the grounds which could be used instead of rooms, such as a Big Oak Tree or the Garden Shed. Objects which represent the weapons can be placed in different parts of the grounds and have to be found. Clues need to be created and hidden in the different areas to explain the whereabouts of each suspected character, which may be school staff! Motives also need to be devised.

Puzzle magazines often have clue-based problems which can be adapted and used for a similar purpose.

Idea 7.19 Digital versus paper maps

When your class is undertaking a walk, compare the experience of using a digital GPS device with a traditional map. Which is easiest to use and which helps you route find the quickest? Does it matter which type of map is used?

Idea 7.20 Walk as the crow flies

When we talk about getting to a destination 'as the crow flies', it means taking the shortest route. Get the children to a look on a map and compare distances as the crow flies to the distance walked on a path or pavement. They could compare distances using the Google Earth ruler tool. Is it possible to walk somewhere as the crow flies? What is the furthest distance you can walk in a straight line in your playground?

Swallows, swifts and house martins all fly south to Africa for the winter. Where would your class end up if they walked south for half an hour?

Idea 7.21 A massive mind map

Mind maps are a visual way of exploring ideas and concepts in any subject area. Although the concept has been around for centuries, in various forms, Tony Buzan popularised the concept. His book *Mind Maps for Kids* is a useful introduction to the process.[3]

---

3 T. Buzan, *Mind Maps for Kids* (Study Skills) (London: Harper Thorsons, 2008).

Children can create large-scale mind maps outside as a group challenge. It is best if they have been introduced to the process of mind mapping as a paper exercise first. From here, they can replace objects for pictures. This may involve using PE equipment or natural resources found outside. Lengths of rope or chalk can be used to create lines radiating out from the centre word or image.

Exploring What's Out There checklist

Have you:

- Gathered together a good variety of props and resources to enable further outdoor explorations to happen?

- Researched online mapping tools which can be used within a lesson or series of lessons?

- Mapped out your outdoor ideas? Look at your project plans and see where a trail or hunt might represent a useful context for learning specific skills or knowledge.

CHAPTER 8

Caring for Nature

This chapter looks at how we can encourage children to care for the places they live in and the plants and animals which live there through:

- Acquiring practical skills through stewardship tasks.

- Teaching specific concepts to help children understand the natural world.

- Modelling appropriate behaviours and actions.

- Giving children opportunities to develop empathy with other living things.

Children view the world differently to adults. As children grow and develop, so does their perspective of – and relationship with – place. This means that activities and approaches to learning outdoors should take account of the developmental needs and ages of your children. Very often, curriculum guidelines are good at providing information on progression of knowledge and understanding – the cognitive aspects of learning. However, the affective aspects of encouraging children to develop a living relationship with nature and the outdoors may be missing.

An emotional and spiritual connection with nature is necessary for children to truly begin to care enough to take the action needed to look after and play their part in restoring the health of our planet. This can be facilitated by adult mentors who develop positive relationships with children and enable them to spend plenty of time playing in wild or semi-wild natural spaces. Many adults can look back and identify a time in middle childhood (aged roughly between six and twelve years) when they had an 'aha!' moment of self-realisation, when they became aware of their connection to the land or felt a strong connection with nature.

When I was just nine years old, I remember standing at the top of a Cumbrian fell. At that moment, I felt a strong affinity for all those hills and the Lake District as a whole. I recollect spending the

rest of that year with my eyes turned towards those hills whenever I played outside or travelled by car, knowing how lucky I was to live there.

Children learn best when supported by knowledgeable and enthusiastic adults. They do not need moralising lectures about caring for the planet and saving the rainforest – I have found this top-down approach to be ineffective. However, adults who model environmentally responsible behaviour, thoughts and actions can make a positive different to how children take care of the world around them. Pick up litter, enjoy beautiful views and be enthusiastic about any plants or animals discovered. Teach your children to treat all wildlife gently and respectfully. Have a look at Chapter 12 for more ideas.

In Sweden, the I Ur och Skur (Rain or Shine) schools,[1] and the outdoor organisation Frilufts-främjandet, have developed a clear progression in outdoor experiences, which takes account of the developmental needs and ages of children and also how they view the world. The recognition of children's right to play in nature, their experience of the outdoor life, learning about land access rights and undertaking increasingly more adventurous activities that encourage greater independence, is well-thought out. The progression of experiences appear to match the developmental

---

1 J. Robertson, *I Ur och Skur, 'Rain or Shine': Swedish Forest Schools*. Creative STAR Learning Company Report (2008). Available at: <http://creativestarlearning.co.uk/wp-content/uploads/2013/06/Rain-or-shine-Swedish-Forest-Schools.pdf>

stages of empathy in early childhood, exploration in middle childhood and personal definition and social responsibility in adolescence, which are outlined by David Sobel in *Childhood and Nature*. [2]

It all begins with babies and toddlers playing and having fun in nature and sharing this delight with parents and adults. At the age of three and four, children are introduced to a fantasy character, called Skogsmulle. He is a unique woodland creature around which stories, games and songs have been created. A Skogsmulle puppet is used for this purpose.

As the children grow older, around five or six, they learn to take care of nature through Skogsmulle. Other fantasy characters – friends of Skogsmulle – are also introduced. The Skogsmulle leaders do not preach environmental action. Instead, drama, games, stories, songs and lots of fantasy and imagination are the vehicle for learning about nature. The use of the Skogsmulle character is central to this approach – Skogsmulle teaches children to cherish nature, because you want to take care of the things you cherish.

As children grow, the emphasis continues on playing in nature, whether this is on a beach, in the forest or in the hills and mountains. Children are also simultaneously introduced to adventurous sports such as skating, sledging and skiing. As children enter middle childhood, the opportunities to explore in the outdoors take greater precedence. This is when campfires are made by children and

2 Sobel, *Childhood and Nature*, p. 20.

organised adventure activities continue. Further groups exist for teenagers which involve expeditions, often in combination with acts of social responsibility.

Free play in the wild

When children are allowed to play freely in a natural space, such as woodland, beaches or moorland, they will tend to use found materials for play purposes – creating miniature worlds, playing with sticks, sorting leaves and so on. This free play in natural spaces helps children to develop a long-term connection with wild places, resulting in an increased likelihood of them developing pro-environmental behaviours and attitudes as adults. [3] For more information on facilitating free play, see Chapter 10.

These days, children are likely to know more about the plants and creatures that live in the Amazon rainforest than those in their garden or local area. Giving children plenty of opportunities to interact with nature on their doorstep helps to address this imbalance.

---

3 N. M. Wells and K. S. Lekies, Nature and the Life Course: Pathways from Childhood Nature Experiences to Adult Environmentalism, *Children, Youth and Environments* 16(1) (2006): 1–24.

If you feel you don't know much about the natural world, don't worry. Most wildlife charities and organisations have lots of helpful resources and advice on their websites, much of which is available for free. It is also worthwhile developing positive relationships with local outdoor and environmental professionals, who often organise training days and activities which you can attend. They can also advise on useful books and resources.

Playing games and using role play helps children to learn more about local wildlife and develops empathy. Encourage children to imagine what it must be like to be a fox or a spider and what skills these animals need to stay alive. Make connections to how children themselves live and survive.

As much as possible, try to link the activities in this chapter to specific teaching concepts or projects – for example, having a short, sharp focus on garden birds if your class is participating in the Royal Society for the Protection of Birds (RSPB) Big Schools' Bird Watch.[4] During this project, look at the biodiversity aspects of your science curriculum and dovetail the work to meet these expectations.

Idea 8.1 Owl ears and listening

Get children to cup their hands (as if scooping up water) and then put the 'cups' behind their ears and listen. Cupped ears collect sound like satellite dishes on the side of your head. This is how owls, rabbits and deer hear.

Listen for the number of birds you can hear around you. Hold up one fist. Every time you hear a new bird call, raise a finger. Try this in different places outside. Ask the children where they think this will work best.

Idea 8.2 Owl eyes

An owl's eyes are fixed in their sockets, so in order to see, they have to move their whole head. To get an idea of what this is like, ask the children to make binoculars by encircling their eyes with their hands and then to look around them. Practice is needed to see the world this way.

Older children can compare their own field of vision to that of an owl. In pairs, they should draw a large-ish circle on the ground. One person stands in the centre, the other behind them on the edge of the circle. The person behind should move slowly around the other in a circle. When the person in the centre can see their moving partner, without moving their head, they should mark this spot on the circumference of the circle. The activity should then be repeated, but the person in the centre should make binoculars around their eyes. The children can then investigate any differences.

---

4 See <http://www.rspb.org.uk/schoolswatch>

Idea 8.3 Bring birds to you

Ask the children to lay a trail of breadcrumbs that lead to a seat where they are sitting. They should watch and wait, keeping very still, and see if they can get a bird to come to them. With classes of children, this works well if they have built their own bird hide. They can set out crumb trails leading to the bird feeding station.

Idea 8.4 Build a nest

Building a nest sounds much easier than it is in reality. In the springtime, birds are busy building nests using local materials within their flight range. It is worth finding out more about the variety of nests that birds make – for example, swallows and house martins use clay or mud, ospreys drop sticks onto old tree tops and blue tits often use nesting boxes.

Challenge children to build group nests, or perhaps a little nest for a toy bird. However, split the class in half. One half of the class should only use clothes pegs to collect and build their nests. After all, birds can only use their beaks to gather materials and build their nests. The other half should use their hands as normal. Compare the end results, and then compare these to the nests birds have made. This activity will really help children to appreciate the nest-building skills of birds.

Idea 8.5 Walk like an animal

Walking like another animal takes practice and makes children walk very slowly. Lift your leg high and place the foot flat on the ground, rolling from the outside to the inside of the foot as you do so. This is a classic stalking movement.

Use this stalking approach to play games that involve creeping about. For example, ask for a volunteer to be a hen guarding her eggs from a predator, such as a fox. Stones can be used to represent the eggs. As it is night-time, and chickens have poor night vision, the hen is blindfolded. Using the stalking movement, the rest of the class take turns to be the fox and creep up and try to remove an egg. The hen should have her eggs close by but is not allowed to touch them. If she hears the fox, she should point in the direction of the sound. For older children, playing this in woodland or on a noisy surface is particularly challenging.

Idea 8.6 Hold an animal parade

Watching birds and other animals, and then miming their specific actions, can help children to understand how other animals move and behave. When in the school grounds or a local space, brainstorm the types of animals you might see in different places. Then go for an animal parade. For example:

- When passing the pond, waddle like a duck.
- Near a park bench, nod like a pigeon.
- Across the playground, swoop like gulls.
- By the wall, stalk like a cat.
- At the lamp post, pretend to pee like a dog.

Idea 8.7 Be inconspicuous

This activity works well for budding spies, soldiers and detectives as well as animal lovers. It's all about trying to make yourself inconspicuous. This is helpful when learning how to watch wildlife.

Ask children for their ideas about how they could be inconspicuous in the playground. After trying out several suggestions, use some animal examples:

- Mice – wearing camouflaged colours.
- Rabbits – blending into the background.
- Spiders on webs – being very still and quiet.

Encourage the children to try and blend into the background by sitting against a tree or under a hedge. The human outline can be broken by putting up a hood or crouching low. The children could also play a game of hide 'n' seek to practise these skills.

Idea 8.8 Still and silent

In the still and silent game, an adult or a chosen child pretends to be a named predator (e.g. a kestrel). The rest of the children start walking around the outdoor space (or do this when going for a walk). When the kestrel calls out 'camouflage', the rest of the group (e.g. mice) must become camouflaged or they will be eaten. The kestrel counts to five and then turns around to see who they can catch moving. Next time, the kestrel only counts to four, then three and so on, until there is no time for the mice to do anything other than freeze.

Afterwards, ask the children whether, if an animal wants to be camouflaged, it is more important to be still or to have the right colours. Camouflage is a concept that has as much to do with stillness and silence as it does colour.

Idea 8.9 Colour sticks and camouflage

Buy or make some coloured lolly sticks and hide them around the outdoor space. Give the children a specific length of time (e.g. three minutes) to find as many sticks as possible. At the end of the allotted time, see which colour sticks the children have found. In theory, the brightly coloured sticks should be easier to find because they are not as well camouflaged. Be warned, you may not get all the dull coloured sticks returned! Matchsticks work well too for this purpose, especially with older children.

This activity is useful prior to looking at photos of different animals and working out what messages colour and pattern send. With older children, you can also link this to what colours and styles are used in clothing and for what purpose (e.g. high-visibility jackets for being seen, wildlife watchers wearing more camouflaged clothes).

Idea 8.10 Adopt an animal

Wildlife charities have recognised for many years that people respond well to campaigns to save one charismatic species. Apply the tactic to learning too. The class can choose a local animal that exists in their area. This can then be used as a focus for examining:

- Adaptations – what characteristics does the species have which enable it to survive?

- Food webs – where does this species sit within a food web? What food does it eat and does it get hunted and/or eaten by others?

- Life cycle – what is the life cycle of this species? Can we see this in action?

- Classification – what type of species is the animal? Find out more about animal taxonomy.

- ■ Habitat – where does this species live and why? Who else lives there? Undertake a SWOT (strengths, weaknesses, opportunities and threats) analysis of the species. Visit the habitat and look for an example. Ask a wildlife expert about any actions which can be taken by the class to look after this species.

- ■ Stories, songs, poems and artwork can all be undertaken to reinforce the scientific learning. Often there is folklore connected with native species.

A useful assessment can be undertaken using drawing and writing. At the start of the project, ask the children to draw the species. What does it look like? Can they annotate their drawing by explaining its particular characteristics? Where does it live? They should draw its habitat and shelter. What does it eat? What else do the children know about this species? At the end of the project, the same activity can be repeated and the results compared.

Idea 8.11 Step forward with wildlife

If the children are particularly interested in farm animals, local wildlife or rainforest creatures, then this activity can be a fun way to find out and reinforce knowledge. Stand at one side of the playground or netball court. A group of children should line up at the other side. Hold up a picture or model of the animal. The children then take turns to say something (e.g. 'It's an owl', 'It likes to hunt at night', 'Its babies are called owlets'). Each child who offers a correct new statement takes one step forward. The first child to reach the other side of the playground is the winner.

Life cycles of animals and plants

Children enjoy practical opportunities to witness the life cycles of plants and animals. Many settings now have chickens, guineas pigs and other animals in residence. Whilst you may not be ready for this type of commitment (yet), consider other temporary ways you could accommodate this work, such as those outlined below.

Idea 8.12 Find and collect frogspawn

Caring for tadpoles and releasing them back into their original pond once they have become froglets is a simple but powerful route into finding out more about life cycles. Seek advice from a local ranger or wildlife expert as to which place is a good place to find spawn and to advise on appropriate ways of collecting and caring for frogspawn. More information can also be found from the Amphibian and Reptile Conservation Trust.[5]

---

5 See <http://www.arc-trust.org>

Idea 8.13 Hatch chickens

There are commercial companies which supply eggs to schools (for a fee). They provide the incubator, fertile eggs and other materials. If possible, look for a reputable local company – usually, there is an agreement that they will collect the equipment and chicks once they have hatched – and check what happens to the chicks afterwards.

Idea 8.14 Create minibeast homes

Whilst there is a growing trend for creating minibeast hotels, which is a very interesting project for reusing unwanted items, nothing beats a good old-fashioned log pile! In the UK there are around nine hundred species of invertebrates which live in or on dead and decaying wood.

Try to include some big logs cut from native trees in the centre, which should remain undisturbed, with smaller, faster-rotting logs arranged around the edges for children to turn over and look under. Have some logs half buried in the ground too. For a more 'refined' log pile, create a stumpery garden. These were popular in Victorian times. It involves making the most of root formations and carefully placing logs vertically into the ground in attractive layouts. The trick is to site any of these artificial homes near long grass, and reasonably close to a hedge or a tree.

Ponds are another great way to attract wildlife – even a small one will bring in birds, amphibians, dragonflies, mammals and reptiles.

Idea 8.15 Put up bird nesting boxes

Make up or buy nest boxes. Ask a local RSPB officer for advice on the most suitable types and locations – certain species of birds need different types of boxes located in different places. Birds also need access to food and water. There is lots of advice on helping birds on the RSPB website.[6] It is also possible to set up webcams in nesting boxes which enable children to observe the chicks live.

Idea 8.16 Raise trout or salmon

It is possible to raise trout or salmon in partnership with a local wildlife or conservation group. In Scotland, there are projects such as Salmon in the Classroom,[7] which involve classes having a hatchery and assisting fisheries trusts in restocking rivers for conservation purposes.

6 See <http://www.rspb.org.uk/advice/helpingbirds>
7 See <http://www.snh.org.uk/salmonintheclassroom>

Idea 8.17 Consider death

Death is an important part of the life cycle of any plant or animal. Be sensitive to cultural and social beliefs about death, but do not be afraid to talk about and respectfully examine any found dead animals, for example, worms, wasps and other minibeasts. This will help children to understand more about life and death, and related traditions, beliefs and customs. Offer an alternative activity for those who do not wish to be involved and check that you are following any school or local guidelines if they exist.

Let children examine plant matter, including flowers, seeds, stems and roots. If a plant in a container dies, keep the plants, which can then be dissected with tweezers and examined under a microscope or lens.

Idea 8.18 Time-lapse videos of decay or change

Create a time-lapse video of a dandelion or other plant – often children do not know that dandelion flowers become dandelion clocks. It can also be interesting for children to put a piece of fruit outside in a place where it will not be disturbed and watch how it decays over several days. Ask them to predict what will happen beforehand.

Sunflowers can be very successful for a project involving taking one photo per day or week. The children observe the plants growing and flowering, then the flowers going to seed. For a complete life cycle, they could collect the seeds and plant them in the spring.

Idea 8.19 Gather seeds and grow them

Gardening is all about life cycles and facilitating them in different ways to our advantage. Suggestions for gardening are given in Chapter 9.

To gather seed collections, get the children to attach double-sided sticky tape to the soles of their shoes or boots and walk through a patch of long, dry grass. Afterwards, the tape can be carefully removed, the seeds picked off with tweezers and planted in top soil. It will be exciting to see what plants grow – the children could help in identifying these.

Idea 8.20 Grow a jungle

Trees usually take a long time to grow but eventually you will have a wood which will be a great resource for children to use. Saplings can be bought at different ages and heights. Depending on the age and tree species, these can be low cost and sometimes even free. For example, the Woodland Trust run a scheme which enables schools to receive free native trees and hedgerow shrubs. Another economical approach is to look for windblown or dropped seeds or berries in the autumn and collect these – for example, helicopter seeds from sycamores, acorns from oaks, berries from hawthorns and nuts from hazels. Seek advice from a local ranger about the best place to plant different trees as some species can be quite fussy. If you have a willow den, the pruned stems can be inserted directly into the ground and will grow.

Food webs and interdependency

There are lots of experiential activities which can be undertaken to help children understand that everything in nature is connected. Introduce the concept of the food chain before the food web. It is important to emphasise that the sun kick-starts the process by providing energy to plants to help them grow through photosynthesis. Stories, such as Celia Godkin's *Wolf Island*,[8] can provide a simple explanation about food chains and how populations of plants and animals are affected.

Idea 8.21 How important is nature?

> Everything in nature is alive in its own way; is on its own adventure, and deserves its own wellbeing. Everything in nature is no more and no less important than anything else.
>
> Colin Mortlock

Is there one animal or plant that is more important than any other? How can the children investigate this question? What evidence will they need to gather when they go out into your school grounds or a nearby greenspace? The children should undertake this challenge in groups and be prepared to report back to the rest of the class.

Idea 8.22 This is your life

This activity can be completed using an animal which is common to your school grounds or local area – for example, a blackbird. Begin by asking the children to think about what a day in the life of a blackbird might be like:

- What activities does it get up to?

- What dangers might it face? How will it avoid or manage these?

---

8 Celia Godkin, *Wolf Island* (Markham, ON: Fitzhenry & Whiteside, 2007).

- What about safe places to go? Where might a blackbird nest?

Next, consider the challenges of being a blackbird, not just for a day but during a whole year. Ask the children what blackbirds have to do to survive. For example:

- Keep warm through winter and find enough food.

- Find a mate and a suitable place to nest.

- Build a nest in spring and sit on the clutch of eggs.

- Find enough food in the summer to feed its young.

Give each pair or group of children a map of the school grounds. Agree symbols to represent different areas, such as:

- The best places to find food (What might that be?)

- Sources of water

- Suitable nesting sites

- Other shelter (e.g. from weather, predators)

- Danger spots (What hazards might a blackbird face?)

- Possible sources of pollution

The groups of children should take the maps outside and look for the different areas, marking these on the map using the agreed symbols. They can also observe the behaviour of blackbirds to find out more information as they do so. Remind them about how to watch birds and appropriate behaviour, such as keeping away from nesting birds.

Back inside, the groups can use the information gathered to create a brief presentation. This might be a story, a song, a short play or something else to perform to other groups.

Idea 8.23 The circle of life

Ask your class to look at this diagram and to discuss it in pairs or trios.

See what ideas the children come up with and take any questions. Then ask them the following questions:

- Where do humans fit in with this diagram?

- How can it be used to explain the interdependency of life? For example, what would happen if the sun didn't shine?

- What would be the impact of introducing new species into the environment (e.g. beavers in some parts of Scotland)?

- Is there anything which should be added or removed from the diagram?

Then ask them to go outside and illustrate the diagram with examples from the school grounds or local area. For example, what is the impact if litter is removed from the school grounds?

Creating and improving habitats

The practical maintenance tasks and fieldwork involved in creating or improving a piece of land, whether it is part of the school grounds or

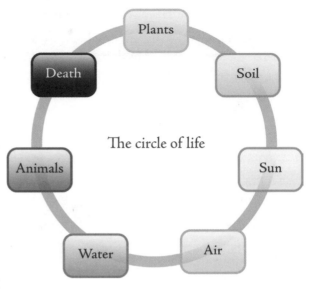

The circle of life

adopting a local patch of ground, ensures that children have first-hand opportunities to observe living things all year round. The experience will help to increase their knowledge about, and understanding of, nature. In addition, it is very satisfying for children to see that their efforts to improve an area have been worthwhile.

Ideally, a whole-school approach works best, where all classes agree to be involved in the process of improving their grounds. It should be a participative approach, as advocated by Learning through Landscapes, the UK school grounds charity. In this way, it is not left to one keen teacher to manage this on top of a high-commitment teaching job. It also means that children can learn about different aspects of the grounds year on year as they move up through the school. Sensory or wildlife gardens are popular in many schools – however, more fun can be had on a large scale if the entire school grounds become wildlife friendly.

If you are the lone teacher, make sure that you can commit to the project on a long-term basis and can integrate this into your ongoing curriculum work. For more information, read a book about wildlife gardening and seek professional advice.

I have written briefly about gardening in Chapter 12. Remember that you must seek your head teacher's permission before making changes to the grounds.

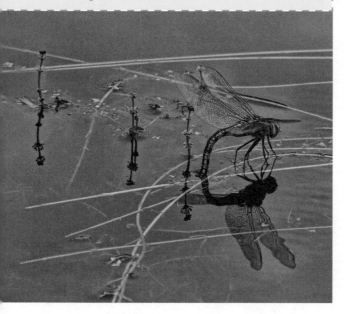

Idea 8.24 What lives in the school grounds?

Develop a database about animals and plants that are found in the school grounds or local area. If this is added to annually, then good comparative records can be built up which can be used for future analysis – but make sure to pick the same times of year to undertake the surveys. Such records can help in monitoring the impact of making your grounds more nature-friendly. Begin small with a focus on one feature or area, such as a log pile or bird-feeding station, rather than the totality of wildlife recorded within the whole grounds.

Idea 8.25 Undertake a John Muir Award

The John Muir Award is an environmental scheme which encourages awareness and responsibility for the natural environment.[9] It can be undertaken by a class from around Year 4 upwards, with a focus on conservation and helping to look after a wild place. The level of the award depends upon the number of hours spent on practical work. The award also involves finding out about John Muir and his life – there is a lovely set of Muir Missions to carry out outside which really makes his life come to life!

Idea 8.26 Feeding birds and providing water

There are lots of options for feeding birds aside from providing commercially bought food. Children can have fun designing their own bird food recipes from ingredients such as suet, seeds, breadcrumbs (preferably wholemeal), apples, pears, blackberries and plums (British fruit), cheese, cooked rice and soaked raisins.

It is important to remember to clean bird tables and feeders regularly to avoid a build-up of harmful parasites and bacteria from old food, which can kill birds. The RSPB also recommends:

■ Keeping an eye on the amount of food being eaten – put out less rather than more so that it is eaten when fresh.

---

9 See <http://www.johnmuiraward.org>

- Moving feeding stations to different locations every few months to stop droppings building up underneath the feeding areas.

- Keeping the feeding areas near to where birds can take cover, such as near hedges or trees.

- Washing your hands after feeding birds.

Birds also need a good supply of rainwater to drink and bathe in. Ponds are best and need not be large. Children can experiment with seeing which types of bowls and water containers birds prefer. Rinse out bird baths and water containers daily, especially in summer months, and allow the containers to dry out before replenishing.

Idea 8.27 Create a mini wildlife garden

What is the smallest wildlife garden that can be created? Some schools give their children a one square metre plot each, but you can experiment with different sizes and models. For example, it is possible to create a pond in a tyre or bucket. You could also consider a terrarium, which is a microversion of a greenhouse.

Idea 8.28 Succession gardens

Succession gardens are the ultimate 'lazy' experiment. Basically, you prepare a patch of bare ground where plants can arrive and self-seed. Your class should monitor which plants arrive and in what quantities. Can they work out where each of the plants has come from? For example, in my garden I have a hawthorn tree and a dog rose bush, both of which grew from seed mostly likely dropped by a passing bird. If you monitor the patch throughout the year, it is possible to see the succession in progress.

Caring for Nature checklist

Have you:

- Thought about how you model environmental behaviours and attitudes? Do you need to work out your approaches to:

  - Handling animals (dealing with spiders, wasps, etc.)?

  - Actively and positively dealing with litter?

  - Use of resources – reusing and recycling as much as possible?

- Considered how to include stewardship opportunities into your ongoing classwork? Focus on little tasks as much as big events.

- Planned projects which teach specific concepts about animals and plants and their role in ecosystems?

- Checked out your class library and built up a collection of books which focus on positive environmental messages and an appreciation of nature and the natural world?

CHAPTER 9

What to do in Concrete Jungles

In an ideal education system, every class would have access to beautiful school grounds that have been carefully designed for play and learning, in consultation with the children, staff and local community. This would include native plants to give the grounds a high biodiversity value, mature trees and bushes, a variety of surfaces, a sandpit big enough for lots of children to play in, a range of water facilities and so on. The reality, in lots of schools, is a grey, flat piece of asphalt and barely a green leaf in sight. It is easy to feel disheartened in this situation.

I find viewing any outdoor space as a blank canvas helps my perspective. It is a place full of potential and possibility. What inspired me to think this way were two Aboriginal women being interviewed on TV several years ago. They were standing in the middle of the Australian bush. The interviewer asked them what they saw in the patch of 'waste ground'. The two women looked at each other and laughed loudly. 'You may see waste ground,' they said, 'but we see one big free supermarket.'

Very often, it is assumed that you need a lovely outdoor space before you can teach children outside. I would suggest that the opposite is true. In order for you and your children to create a lovely outdoor space, you need to have spent time working and playing there in all its unloveliness, and in all weathers and seasons.

It is only by using your grounds that you will begin to understand the space better and will be able to make informed decisions about what improvements are needed. Lots of the ideas in this book work well in concrete jungles, especially with the odd tweak here and there.

Think about what you have

Firstly, start by going out and looking at what you *do* have outside. Take a 3D approach: look at the buildings and sky above, the surface below and the walls and fences around you. Here are some of the structures I've discovered by doing this – and some strategies to exploit them.

Idea 9.1 Drainpipes

Some drainpipes are tough enough to take a rope line. They can also work well for work around pulleys and long thin vertical displays of artwork. Those which aren't so sturdy (do check) can be used as information stations where notices can be attached – most have a gap between the pipe and the wall.

Idea 9.2 Gates

Gates make great miniature work stations and they can be a very identifiable space for a group. I've had children successfully undertake weaving projects, create water walls and carry out other experimental activities using gates. If you have a gate near a busy road, then it is a sign of responsibility that you trust a group to work there safely. What measures will they, and you, put in place to enable them to work there safely?

Idea 9.3 Fences

Fences come in many shapes and forms. Use S-hooks, karabiners and Velcro to attach objects or hang bags up. There are all sorts of planters which can be attached to fences too. For example, try growing daffodil bulbs in welly boots which can be hung up – just make a hole in the top of the boot to attach a string and another one in the foot to allow water to drain out.

Idea 9.4 Give your ugly fence a makeover

Fences lend themselves to a variety of art projects and interactive displays. If your school has lots of ugly fencing, then challenge your class to give it a makeover.

- How can one class brighten up a big area quickly?
- Should the project be a permanent feature? If so, is permission needed and from whom?
- How will the artwork be maintained or will it be a temporary installation?

Idea 9.5 Shelters

Shelters often have posts which can be used in different ways. For example, put a rope between two posts and create a den with a piece of tarpaulin. Washing lines can be added to attach objects and to use as a display. Challenge your class to think of ideas to make the place more welcoming and comfortable.

Idea 9.6 Nooks and crannies

Nooks and crannies are those little spaces tucked away, such as around the back of a mobile classroom, in-between a wall and a shed or a bush big enough for a children to hide under. These work well for imaginative thinking around who might live there. The atmosphere within these spaces also helps with scene-setting in writing.

Idea 9.7 Cracks

Cracks in pavements and walls can be viewed in interesting ways. Create a 'cracking good story': this involves looking for cracks, lines and weathering, and telling the story of how the wall or pavement came to look like that. Alternatively, children may see different images within the patterns made by cracks – I once found a map of Australia made by paint peeling off a wall. Children also love the idea of placing plastic toy eyes in cracks and crevices to peer out. After all, you never know who is watching you these days!

Idea 9.8 The aspect

If your grounds are north of your building, then they will get a lot less sun than south-facing grounds. Use this knowledge to your advantage when investigating weather at different times of year. North-facing areas are great on a hot day for a bit of shade and useful in winter for finding lingering ice and snow. Likewise, plant shade-loving plants in north-facing grounds and sun-loving plants in south-facing areas.

Idea 9.9 Windows and doors

Mathematically, windows and doors are divine! They often have shapes within shapes – what looks like four panes of glass may actually be five squares and four rectangles. Which window has the most shapes within it?

For older children, measuring the length and width of windows and doors and their features can help determine whether they fit the proportions of the golden ratio. If so, are they more aesthetically pleasing than those which do not?

Idea 9.10 Walls

Some outdoor walls have more potential than others. The trend for smooth, rendered featureless walls, commonly seen on new school buildings, means they lack the quirkiness of older walls. However, just give them a tap. If you get a funny echoing sound, then use this for exploring the ability of a building to transmit sounds. Teach the children about the Morse code and then ask them to explore the exterior walls as a medium for sending Morse code messages to each other. How well does this work?

Victorian buildings can tell you a lot about what local stone was available and how it was designed and built. Invite a geologist, architect or historian to give you their perspective on your school buildings. You and the children will be amazed at their knowledge and the secrets of your school walls.

Idea 9.11 Surfaces

Aside from the different textures of walls and the ground, drainage features introduce additional surface options. Here are some suggestions for a texture hunt:

- Use paper and crayons for taking rubbings.
- Use calico cotton and experiment with different plants. For the best effect, create a line pattern on a six-inch square of calico using masking tape. Then take the cotton square outside. Look for common weeds, soil, berries and leaves and rub them into different parts of the fabric, creating an array of different coloured shapes between the masking tape lines. By also pressing the cotton onto different surfaces when the natural materials are rubbed onto the cotton, an imprint of the surface is also made. Remove the masking tape when finished and enjoy the colourful pattern that has emerged.

- Try pressing clay onto different surfaces and looking at the imprint.
- Tin foil rubbed onto different surfaces creates an interesting effect and can be used during or after wet weather.

Idea 9.12 Apply grey matter to grey matter

Another starting point is to take your class outside and, in pairs, ask them to brainstorm all the ideas they can think of for learning in this particular space. Children of all ages will have a number of innovative suggestions. Be warned, if it is during or after wet weather, this will involve jumping in puddles!

With older children, you can assign them topic- or subject-related activities. Alternatively, list the curriculum areas and see what they come up with. Which curriculum area do they find most lends itself to an asphalt space?

Idea 9.13 Import natural materials

Many outdoor activities work well with natural materials. Consult a friendly ranger and find out where your class can gather natural materials within walking distance of the school. Other alternatives include putting a call out to parents. One school asked every child to bring back two stones from their holidays after the summer. Just remember to request that everything is gathered in line with the land access laws in your country.

You can also buy many natural materials. However, the level of ownership is much higher when children have invested time and effort in sustainably gathering the resources. This helps them value the resources and activities which use them.

Idea 9.14 Mapping microclimates

There can be a real mix of windy and sheltered spots in built-up areas: often the wind will funnel between two buildings, puddles will form in dips and the run-off from gutters in rainy weather can be magnificent to observe. Make it an ongoing class experiment to find out which parts of the grounds are the windiest, most sheltered, wettest, driest and so on, and build up a map of interesting areas. This is microclimatology in action!

Idea 9.15 Does life exist in a concrete jungle?

Whether life exists on hard surfaces could be a matter of debate in the classroom. Children could find out what life forms exist and where. Spiders and other minibeasts may be sheltering in a crack

in the pavement or a crevice in a wall. This would be a good time to consider how to care for such animals – primarily, the need to leave them in peace or return them to where they were found.

Often weeds can be found growing in all sorts of nooks and crannies. This would be an opportunity to discuss the notion that 'a weed is a plant growing in the wrong place'. What would be the right place? Says who?

Idea 9.16 Make the space a fan-ta-stick place to learn

Using sticks for maths and other number work is particularly effective in built-up spaces. When tapping sticks, the sound is magnified and the children tend to enjoy the multisensory approach. The majority of the maths posts on my blog involve the use of sticks.[1]

Exploring rhythms through the use of sticks outside works well too. If your school has a music teacher, then use their experience and knowledge to help you plan some rhythm work. There are now a variety of recording apps for digital devices which enable the recording of sounds or performances.

---

1 See <http://creativestarlearning.co.uk/>

Idea 9.17 Create an outdoor dressing-up box

Dressing up works well for free play during breaktimes or within class times, particularly when children can access them freely. Role-play costumes are not needed – it is better that children learn to improvise through the use of cast-off clothing and a variety of found materials. For example:

- Pieces of fabric can be wrapped around the body in lots of different ways. Many cultures have their own styles – for example, the original kilt is a length of tartan wrapped in a particular way to create the garment.

- Accessories such as unwanted hats, scarves, umbrellas, bags and belts.

- Simple capes – these are popular with older as well as younger children.

- Quick-dry or waterproof items for using on wet or snowy days.

- Spare outdoor wet weather clothing.

- A wheeled suitcase for storing the dressing-up items. This can be a play item in its own right too.

Do not feel the need to keep an outdoor dressing-up box fastidiously clean or tidy. The golden rule is not to pack away wet items. For this reason, quick-drying dressing-up items are best. Remember to check any donated items of second-hand clothing, especially the pockets, prior to putting in the box. Who knows what treasure may be found!

Idea 9.18 Start developing the school grounds

Asphalt is expensive stuff – it costs a lot of money to put down and also to break it up and replace it. The cheaper alternative is to put interesting features on top of it. This also allows for greater experimentation, especially if objects aren't permanently attached to the surface – you can move around planters, seats and other features until you get a layout that works.

But children do need access to nature. Naturalised school grounds positively impact on children's well-being and provide greater opportunities for creative and imaginative play. It is also much better for wildlife, especially if you focus on biodiversity.

Planters and raised beds work well when greening and zoning a grey outdoor space. One urban nursery I visited had created a massive raised bed which was used to plant up a small wood! It gave a great sense of wildness and children enjoyed the raised level of the paths and the feeling of height.

Using natural materials, such as stones, bark chips, sand, soil and water, helps naturalise the most urban of outdoor spaces. These materials can all be put on top of asphalt too.

Idea 9.19 Get gardening

The easiest way to get gardening happening, and which allows every child a chance to experience it, is to introduce raised beds, window boxes and other forms of container planting. The type of container will depend on your funds and the likelihood of vandalism occurring. Big sturdy planters are needed in some schools. Others may go for makeshift planters such as welly boots and old milk bottles, which can be taken in and out daily and go home over the holidays.

Buy a basic kids gardening book and have fun following the ideas and suggestions. Remember to take account of the school holidays interrupting the growing season. As your own confidence grows, you can expand the amount of gardening you undertake with your class.

Always garden organically as much as possible, which means avoiding using chemicals. There are many ways to deal with pests and weeds which do not involve using pesticides or herbicides. Avoid peat-based compost. Very often, your local authority landscaping service will be able provide topsoil at a very competitive price.

One of the biggest challenges is integrating gardening into an overstuffed curriculum. This can be mitigated in two ways. Firstly, adapt your garden so that it links in with a theme or project you are undertaking. For example:

- Farming/agriculture – grow crops.
- Second World War – create a Dig for Victory garden.
- Romans – research and grow herbs that the Romans are known to have used.
- Friendship – look at complementary plants which thrive when grown together.
- Victorians – plant heritage vegetable crops.
- Art – design a rainbow garden using plants of different colours.
- Minibeasts – plan a garden suitable for as many wild creatures as possible.

Secondly, link the maintenance into ongoing work and consider where it would fit into the curriculum. For example, writing instructions about how to plant and care for a vegetable garden could be part of a functional writing task. Harvesting food and cooking it could be part of a home economics project. Weeding the raised bed offers a chance to examine plant structures for a science lesson. It is worth planning these activities in advance – have a look at Chapter 12 for more information.

Idea 9.20 Guerrilla gardening

Guerrilla gardening is a concept that has been floating around since the 1970s, but it has recently come to wider attention. It is about illegally greening neglected spaces, usually in cities. These can be tiny patches of ground, such as around a lamp post or at a street corner, which people plant up with flowers or vegetables.

The concept can work well in schools too, especially old schools or ones that are due to be closed or substantially refurbished. Help children to find out more about guerrilla gardening – searching for images online can be a good place to start. Next, go outside and see what parts of the school grounds could be brightened up with a little bit of temporary planting. Some families that garden at home may have cuttings, spare plants, seeds or bulbs which could be donated. A local garden centre may also be willing to donate bedding plants. As with any practical work, put in place a maintenance plan so that the plants get looked after.

This could also be a good opportunity to grow some plants for the children to eat or which would attract wildlife. What you grow will depend on your soil type, climate and aspect, but reliable and fast-growing vegetables include salad leaves, spinach, Chinese greens, carrots and dwarf beans. To ward off pests in an environmentally friendly way, you could companion plant with nasturtiums, marigolds or alliums (all of which are also edible). If you have a warm, sheltered spot with free-draining soil then you could try herbs like thyme, sage or lavender. To attract bees and butterflies, try planting sedums or buddleia. You will find lots of information on the Internet if you need more advice.

Idea 9.21 Leave a positive legacy through art

Artwork can be used to create a positive legacy. If each child who graduates from your school has been involved in some form of collaborative artwork, this leaves a reminder of the child's time and presence in the school.

Consider art projects that will leave a lasting contribution in the school grounds. These can reflect local cultures and traditions, children's interests and ongoing project work. For example:

- A bench painted and decorated by a class which can be touched up annually by subsequent classes.
- An entrance mosaic or plaque that exemplifies the school's values.
- A sculpture completed by a class working alongside a professional artist.
- A mural designed and painted by the children.
- A playtime box of art materials, ideas and activities for use outside, along with a system for managing this.

The main consideration with any permanent artwork outside is to have a plan for maintaining (or removing) the work when it begins to look shabby.

If you cannot lift a leaf without permission

If you work in a new-build school with tight regulations about what changes and activities can be undertaken outside, then begin a positive dialogue with the janitors and managers about what is possible. It can take time to build a relationship.

Keep the focus on the benefits for the children and the need for learning to happen outside. Rephrase questions to make the discussions solution-focused – for example, rather than asking, 'Can we have a sand pit outside?' try, 'Where do you think the best place would be to put a sand pit outside?' and ensure that the grounds managers understand why it will make such a positive difference.

It also helps to ask for advice: 'I know you appreciate how much the children need daily contact with nature, so I'm wondering what you think would be the best way of getting a bit more greenery into this outdoor space?'

If you work in a school with a particularly constrictive ethos, don't give up. Try the following:

- ■ If you can't use chalk outside, then collect bags of twigs, sticks, stones and cones which can be used for making temporary lines.

- String tends to blow about, so have lengths of rope available for line work.

- Raid your gym cupboard. Very often, PE equipment is deemed more acceptable for outdoor work by those with traditional views on the curriculum and how children should be taught.

- A bag of sand placed on a tarpaulin will do for a 'leave no trace' sand pit. For group work, have several bags of sand on several tarpaulins.

- Create a portable system so that resources can be put out and moved back inside as necessary. Much of my own work uses this type of system – I rely on bags that children can carry, a rucksack and old suitcases for transporting resources.

- Create risk–benefit assessments for all the outdoor work you plan to do. It is really hard to argue with a piece of paper – it doesn't answer back. Do your research about issues which crop up and put measures in place to manage them. Ask others for advice if necessary.

- Find people who share your determination and enthusiasm. Remember that parents and carers can be an asset too.

- Use temporary tubs and containers for gardening projects.

- Ensure any outdoor artwork is beautiful and transient.

Idea 9.22 Adopt your local greenspace

Even within very urban areas there will be natural places within walking distance that can be used regularly off-site – for example, community woodland, beaches and council-managed areas of ground. Local ranger services can be very helpful. It is also worth trying old folk's homes that have large gardens.

There are many advantages to doing this, including:

- Children get to know their local area and community.

- Children have direct contact with nature.

- It is a change of place, which can be as good as a rest.

- Children learn how and where to cross roads safely and develop the habit of walking.

- Children may be able to visit the place outside school with their family and friends.

- They can learn how to look after a piece of ground. This could dovetail nicely with a John Muir Award (see Idea 8.25).

Taking a play-based approach

Even for schools in the most built-up areas, or with run-down playgrounds, it is worthwhile looking at play-based approaches to learning outdoors. National play organisations, such as Play England, Play Scotland and so on, have materials and guidance for schools on different aspects of play and will be able to direct you to local play organisations.[2]

Training and support services are also available to schools to improve school achievement through play. In particular, the Outdoor Play and Learning (OPAL) model [3], developed by Michael Follett, a former play adviser for Gloucestershire Council, has been nationally recognised for its robust approach to supporting school improvement through play. [4]

Many play workers are experienced at developing environments for free-play sessions with groups of children. They can be invited to work with you to model the process or they may be able to lead sessions with your class, and will usually bring along a selection of open-ended resources. You may have to pay for this service, as they mostly work for local charities that operate on a shoestring, but it can help to kick-start the process.

If your school includes Forest School sessions within the curriculum, then this can also be a way of making time and space for free play in a natural setting. This is because it is a child-centred approach rather than a content-driven one. Forest School is defined as 'an inspirational process that offers ALL learners regular opportunities to achieve and develop confidence and self-esteem through hands-on learning experiences in a woodland or natural environment with trees.'[5]

Idea 9.23 Observe the children in your class at play

If we want a child-centred curriculum, then we need to look at what interests and motivates children outside. Going for a walk around at playtime can lead to some useful insights as to what children like to do, so take the opportunity to observe your children playing outside.

- What sort of activities do they get up to?

- Which parts of the playground are being used and for what purpose?

- How does the landscape of the outdoor space affect the play which takes place? Is it flat and featureless or does it have a wide variety of places and spaces? How are children interacting with the landscape?

---

2 See <http://playengland.org.uk>

3 See <http://www.outdoorplayandlearning.org.uk>

4 S. Lester, O. Jones and W. Russell, *Supporting School Improvement through Play: An Evaluation of South Gloucestershire's Outdoor Play And Learning Programme* (London: National Children's Bureau, 2011). Available at: <http://www.playengland.org.uk/media/340836/supporting-school-improvement-through-play.pdf>

5 See <http://www.forestschoolassociation.org/what-is-forest-school>

- What 'loose parts' are available for the children to play with (see Idea 9.26)?

- What gender and age differences exist in the play observed? How is this affected by the available resources, zoning and layout of the grounds?

- What rules exist – both formal and informal – and how do these impact on play? This is a useful follow-up discussion to have with children.

- What curriculum targets or outcomes are being met informally through the free play you see? Do these still need to be officially taught? Can it lessen the demands on class time?

- Are children playing as you would expect or do you see differences compared to being in the classroom? For example, are certain children more sociable or happier outside?

Idea 9.24 Use playtime observations to plan formal learning activities

Using the outdoor space for formal learning can take time, but using a play-based approach can assist with the adjustment process for both adults and children. This includes time at the start of a session to run, explore and relax. Often activities such as scavenger hunts (see Ideas 7.10, 7.11 and 7.12) can be good starters and will appeal to many children's natural curiosity.

I recently observed some six-year-olds with additional support needs who made me realise that they were looking for opportunities to use their whole bodies to swing, balance and gain a different perspective through being at different heights. This led to a series of activities which involved creating rope swings, bridges and challenges which stimulated a high level of engagement from almost all the children.

Share your observations with the children in your class and see what results in terms of potential outdoor activities based upon playtime games. For some suggestions, have a look at the ideas based on the children and nature design principles (see Idea 10.17).

Idea 9.25 Ensure all children in your class get out to play every day

In schools where there are lots of rules and restrictions around play, you may need to seize an opportunity for play when it arises. For example:

- Letting children out to play as soon as the weather improves. You can use this as a springboard to formal work outside or inside.

- Collecting wet weather gear for use in class times (see Idea 2.15).

- Ensuring that every child has a right to play in your class regardless of their behaviour or ability to complete classwork. Alternative strategies include:

■ Discussing the matter with the child and taking a shared solution-focused approach. There could be good reasons why a child is not managing their work or behaviour in class time. If necessary, ask the child's parent or carer for their support. Very often, regular positive dialogue between home and school makes a huge difference.

■ Adjusting your expectations (but keeping them high) of what a child can do, say or complete in terms of classwork.

■ If your school has timetabled options where children choose their activity for part of the day, then consider offering outdoor free-play sessions, especially if you have loose parts available for children to use (see Idea 9.26).

Idea 9.26 Learn through loose parts

Loose parts are a motley collection of open-ended items which children can use in their play or during formal learning activities. Most of the resources are unwanted bits and pieces, such as guttering, fish boxes, computer keyboards, tyres, suitcases and other items that have been donated by parents and local businesses. Occasionally, a few bought items are also added such as tarpaulins. Large natural materials, like wooden discs cut from felled trees or big wooden poles, can be sourced through local timber suppliers. Some councils have systems in place where schools can access wood from their landscape or tree services. The choice and possibilities of resources are endless.

Loose parts enable the most boring outdoor space to come alive, with children showing high levels of creativity and imagination. Because the resources are not toys with a fixed purpose, the children find lots of different ways of using them. However, this means that a class or school which decides to develop a collection of loose parts needs to adopt a process of introduction and a system of management, supervision and use. Undertaking a risk–benefit assessment (see Idea 2.12) about the loose parts is strongly recommended as a way of helping you and the children to think through the issues around their use, managing any identified risks and making the most of the resources.

Children can be involved in sourcing materials – this can be very empowering as they will have greater ownership over the project. It is also an opportunity to explain to parents what is happening and why, and to get them on board. This is important, so they know the benefits of using loose parts. If children and parents are able to see a loose parts play project in action, either by visiting another school or watching a video, they will understand what is needed.

When new and donated materials arrive in school, make sure the items are suitably robust. Some items may need preparatory work – for example, computer keyboards will need the wires chopped off. Set up a system for checking incoming resources and preparing them for use. Some local scrap stores can process material for you and ensure it is safe.

You will need a container or somewhere to store these items. Make sure this is quickly and easily accessible by children to facilitate the tidying-up process. You will also have to put in place a maintenance system which ensures that ongoing tasks take place, such as removing broken items, drying wet clothes and materials, and ensuring a supply of new bits and pieces to replace those which are lost through wear and tear.

When introducing loose parts for the first few times, it helps to have an initial discussion with the class. I lay the items out along the edge of the playground for the children to see, feel and hold. I choose a key item, such as a big bore pipe, and then ask the children for their thoughts about what they think they will need to remember when using this resource. The children will come up with a variety of suggestions – for example, one hazard with bore pipes is holding onto the rim when being rolled around inside the pipe. The children need to know to keep their hands inside the pipe otherwise they risk hurting their fingers. I then ask for suggestions about other resources and the children's advice about how to use them safely.

I make sure that any other specifics are covered too. I have a list of points to address which include matters such as:

- Checking wooden items for splinters and having sandpaper available for children to sand down any rough patches.

- Shouting a consistent warning if a resource accidentally comes flying towards another child – normally this is a rolling tyre!

- Being aware of others, especially when carrying big items – it is everyone's responsibility to be aware.

Once you and the class have agreed expectations around the use of the loose parts, let your children experiment. Watch them play with the resources. It is important that adults avoid interrupting children at play. Intervention should only happen if absolutely necessary. The aim is to encourage children to play independently without needing adult input to do this.

Afterwards, review the session with the children and find out what they thought they learned through their play. In my experience, a lot of technology-based learning arises naturally. Children learn through trial and error about how to construct dens, guttering runs and time machines! They will spend a lot of time fine-tuning their creations to make them work and demonstrate commitment and persistence in finding solutions to design problems.

Much greater degrees of problem-solving, creativity, imaginative play, cooperation and socialisation are often observed than before loose parts were introduced. You can link this work back to the curriculum, thereby reducing the need for formal lessons to cover particular curriculum targets.

Key skills can be taught and practised between sessions. For example, it could be that the children need to learn how to tie knots or develop their skills in lashing poles together for den building. Some children may want to develop a 'tinkering area', inside or out, where items such as old clocks can be taken apart and put back together again.

Having access to an abundant selection of loose parts can be helpful for a wide range of learning activities in any outdoor space. By choosing carefully the props and resources available, you can steer the free play in different directions. For example, having canisters of water, guttering and pipes may lead to investigations around the movement and flow of water. If your school has a nursery class, they may be willing to lend you some of their outdoor play equipment from time to time too.

Whilst I have discussed loose parts as a specific class project, many schools have introduced loose parts into their lunchtimes as part of a whole-school approach to play. The Scrapstore Playpod® is a well-thought out and comprehensive approach which includes lunchtime staff gaining formal play qualifications.[6]

This Place is Like a Building Site is a useful free booklet which outlines the loose parts process taking in three North Lanarkshire Schools.[7] It provides lots of practical advice about training and lists useful resources.

Grounds for Learning have a Scottish Government-funded natural play project which uses an effective combination of developing natural play features, such as sand pits, vegetation, changes in topography and making water available, in tandem with introducing loose parts. *The Good School Playground Guide* gives helpful advice and information and is a 'must-read' if you are considering a whole-school approach.[8]

Idea 9.27 Use loose parts for specific lessons

Over the past few years, I have found myself increasingly using loose parts and natural materials during class time as part of a formal lesson. Children enjoy devising their own challenges and team-building activities using loose parts – capitalise on the creativity which emerges when working with these resources.

Here are some examples of ideas which have arisen from such sessions:

- What is the minimum number of tyres your group can use to cross the playing field without touching the grass?

- Is it possible to transport five litres of water from one side of the playground to the other without any being spilled or wasted? Find the easiest way and also a more interesting or complex way of doing this.

---

6 See <http://www.playpods.co.uk>

7 North Lanarkshire Council, *This Place is Like a Building Site! A Report on the Introduction of Loose Materials to Three Primary Schools in North Lanarkshire* (n.d.). Available at: <http://www.playlink.org/pubs/This_place_is_like_a_building_site.pdf>

8 Learning through Landscapes, *The Good School Playground Guide: Developing School Playgrounds to Support the Curriculum and Nurture Happy, Healthy Children* (n.d.). Available at: <http://www.ltl.org.uk/pdf/The-Good-School-Playground-Guide1382978938.pdf>

■ Design a fun obstacle course for another group to complete. What are the essential and desirable criteria for a fun obstacle course?

Idea 9.28 Use play as a springboard to a series of structured learning activities

Young children who are just beginning to access the formal curriculum find free-play sessions helpful, as they build on the play-based approach taken in many pre-school settings. Older children who struggle with formal approaches to learning will often readily engage in free play with loose parts, so it can be used as a strategy to support them to access the curriculum.

We often have a tendency to jump straight into a learning activity without first having given children a chance to play with materials or explore a resource in their own way. Giving children time to freely play with resources may be a necessary prerequisite to constructive learning experiences. It can help children to explore and learn about the properties of different objects. This can be a good use of time, in that children will come up with their own ideas and suggestions for activities, which can then be developed and extended in different ways. Here is an example of a series of lessons which began with a play session.

Play session with tarpaulin

This session begins with a general discussion about the practicalities of using tarpaulin and how it can be used in different ways. We agree working boundaries and behaviour expectations. After the free-play session, during which I observe and facilitate, we discuss what worked well and what could be even better. Sometimes I show photos from the session and ask the children to explain what is happening. From here, ideas about future activities are formed.

Introducing team challenges that use tarpaulin

Children will have ideas for team-based activities using tarpaulin. Sometimes we all pick one challenge and at other times we each choose different challenges. We may begin with problem-solvers, such as finding the smallest area of tarpaulin that a group can safely stand on. This is usually followed by an activity, such as den building, with a specific focus. For example:

■ Make a den which can fit the whole group standing underneath.

■ Make a den which demonstrates the use of specific knots.

■ Make a den which involves everyone in the group working together.

We show our dens to each other and celebrate everyone's efforts. Afterwards, we will reflect using a review activity.

Extending the skills learned and applying them more widely

For extension activities, we will do a little more preparation beforehand. We might research examples of dens online. We might design our dens on paper, such as making a floor plan. We might create a den using different available materials for comparative reasons – for example, using space/thermal blankets is a completely different experience to using tarpaulin. Time to share findings and reflect is also built in. As a summary, the children may decide to write an advice note to others about the best way to create a den.

Idea 9.29 Begin formal lessons with play-based experiences

In recent years, I have found that beginning a session with a bit of investigative play adds value and interest to a lesson. For example, I have sets of measuring sticks (these are sold as a maths pack). I began by using the sets to make one square metre, which is the suggested use on the website. However, I quickly realised that this was making the learning quite closed. Instead, I now ask groups of children to explore and play with the stick set and come up with their own ideas for how it could be used. This has led to a wide range of purposeful activities related directly to how children think, do and learn. Examples include:

- A game of mathematical hide 'n' seek, where children take turns to hide and find pairs of sticks which are then used for quick mental calculations.

- The sticks are used to create a fraction wall.

- A long jump where the sticks are used to measure the distance jumped.

- Challenges based around creating shapes with specific areas and perimeters.

- Investigating and calculating the maximum height that can be achieved when the sticks are stacked on top of each other.

What has been particularly interesting is listening to the conversations taking place within groups. You hear high level thoughts being expressed about different mathematical concepts and a lot of mental calculations. I have also undertaken this approach with children who have additional support needs. Each time, the creativity and level of mathematical understanding demonstrated by the children has surpassed the teacher's expectations.

What to do in Concrete Jungles checklist

Have you:

- Gone for a walk around your concrete jungle? Look at some of the ideas in this chapter and see what might work in your school.

- Revisited play as part of your professional development? There is a growing body of play literature and research which has relevance to schools and educators, beyond the Early Years.

- Observed your class at breaktimes? Use these observations to help you plan outdoor learning experiences based upon the children's interests.

- Looked at ways of greening your grounds? This is most effective when a participatory approach is used which truly involves children in all aspects of the change process and subsequent maintenance work.

CHAPTER 10

Keeping the Momentum Going

Once you have been outside several times within a short space of time with your class, there will come a point where you need to expand and develop your practice. It is very easy to get stuck in a rut of doing just one type of outdoor activity, or only using one corner of your playground, because it works.

It is important not to get sucked into looking for ideas simply to demonstrate that you are undertaking outdoor learning with your class. If you aren't careful, the purpose and relevance of the activities to the children can become secondary. We know that relevance of learning is crucial. Children will be more motivated and engaged in learning if it is purposeful and not for the sake of ticking the 'outdoor learning' box.

There are lots of ideas that you can adapt to transform your practice. Looking at how children's skills, habits and confidences are developed can help. Through trial and error, teachers can become more judicious about what works and what doesn't in their own practice.

As much as possible, create learning opportunities which:

- Identify and solve real-world problems.
- Can be used comparatively (e.g. with another school elsewhere or year on year or through the seasons).
- Involve an investigation, exploration or challenge – these can be fun or quirky as well as serious. What matters is that you know the concepts and skills that children need to be taught to do the activity.
- Enable children to express their thoughts, feelings and opinions in different ways.
- Provide a real-life illustration of a concept – after all, that's one of the main reasons for being outside.
- Enable practical skills to be acquired and developed.
- Involve your class in devising these tasks – taking on board their interests and ideas can be very empowering.
- Are open-ended and allow children flexibility in how they approach their learning.

Hitting the wall

Marathon runners are well aware of the wall. It happens when the body runs out of its reserves of glycogen and has to start burning fat to obtain energy, which doesn't happen as easily as burning carbohydrate. Runners suffer from fatigue and will find it particularly hard at this point in the race.

Hitting the wall can also happen when embedding the outdoors into your teaching. You can reach a point where you are drained of ideas and may have to deal with various obstacles to working outside on a frequent and regular basis. You are literally running on empty and at this point it is easy to retreat indoors.

This happened to me when I made the move from teaching outside weekly to daily. I was working part-time as an additional support for learning teacher, mainly focusing on maths and literacy work. I didn't have enough material to keep me going and I felt, consequently, that the quality of my teaching deteriorated. I hadn't yet got into the habit of thinking outdoors naturally and I didn't have the time I needed to plan more strategically.

I needed a few strategies to help me through this phase. These are my suggestions for keeping going when the going gets tough – outdoor cheat sheets!

Idea 10.1 Why indoors?

Flip your thinking. Every time you sit down to do your planning, ask 'Why indoors?' Spend a couple of minutes thinking about the outdoor possibilities of everything you intend to do. Do the same with your routines:

- Do you have to register your children inside each morning? Could the day begin outside?

- Will you save time if the children meet you outside after break and check in at the gathering circle?

- Could the school hold assemblies outside from time to time?

Idea 10.2 Think about the totality of the learning experience

Rather than trying to plan big lessons, consider breaking up a longer session with a chunk of outdoor activity. A little and often is sometimes preferable, especially during cold or inclement weather. Bear in mind that outdoor activities can happen:

- As a springboard prior to working back inside or to kick-start a project (e.g. as a stimulus for writing).

- In the middle of a series of lessons (e.g. to gather evidence during a scientific enquiry).

- At the end of a series of activities (e.g. an outdoor event such as sports day or a garden party).

- As a series of outdoor undertakings in their own right, within a subject or across disciplines.

Remember that the indoor and outdoor work should complement each other.

Idea 10.3 Spend time developing year-on-year activities

When starting out, put your time and effort into activities which you will be able to use repeatedly. For example, on my maths courses, we look at ways of using sticks and stones to embed addition and subtraction facts at all levels. Once you get the idea, it doesn't matter what age or stage you teach, the same principles can be applied.

Some areas of the curriculum naturally lend themselves to outdoor work. A good example is measurement. If your class is learning about area, for example, then spend time developing two or three activities which will help the class to understand this concept.

Idea 10.4 Use stories as springboards to outdoor activities

Whether from folklore, legends, fairy tales, novels or picture books, stories provide food for the imagination. Many books are based in outdoor settings or have references to themes such as journeys and explorations which lend themselves to outdoor activities. For example:

- The *Harry Potter* books by J. K. Rowling have lots of references to native trees and plants. This could lead to the planting of a 'Harry Potter hedge' or a 'wand woodland' which includes the trees mentioned in the books from which wands are made.

- The *Scaredy Squirrel* series by Melanie Watt focuses on perceived dangers encountered in different places. This could be followed up by children exploring the school grounds for different risks for a squirrel and suggestions for a first-aid kit that the squirrel might need.

It could also lead to research about red squirrels and ways of making the grounds more wildlife friendly.

■   The Narnia novels, such as *The Lion, the Witch and the Wardrobe*, by C. S. Lewis have elements of fantasy lands. Possible activities which may arise could include creating miniature worlds outside that require a particular method to enter. This could be linked to other literature such as Robert Louis Stevenson's poem 'The Land of Counterpane' or *Alice's Adventures in Wonderland* by Lewis Carroll.

Idea 10.5 Have books and other texts readily available for reading outside

Some children like to read at playtimes or are happy to find a nook or cranny outside in which to settle down and read if they have a spare moment during class time. Books do get more worn outside but take this as an indication that they are being well-used! Some useful considerations also include:

■   Think about places where books can be easily stored and retrieved by the children – this might be a basket, a box or bag system. Find out which the children prefer.

■   Use 'expendable' books outside – ones which don't matter if they get worn or damaged. Ask for donations from parents, pick up old books at jumble sales, etc.

■   Laminate old books to extend their shelf life and make them more resistant to rain and dirt.

■   Allow books to move between the classroom and outdoors, so children make the connection between the two areas and the reading can be continued inside or out.

Idea 10.6 Create outdoor book bags

Many schools use book bags as a literacy-based context for learning at home or school. They are created around popular themes or topics, such as Africa or space. The book bags usually contain a couple of books, a prop (such as a game or cuddly toy) and some suggested activities that are related to the theme of the bag. Book bags can be created for use by a child at home or solely for use in schools to support project work.

As you update or introduce book bags, include an outdoor activity. For example, in an African book bag, this might be the materials and instructions needed to play Dara, a traditional Nigerian strategy game which is normally played outside.

Other suggestions for book bags include:

■   Ideas and resources for writing outside.

- Advice about where and how to share the stories (e.g. reading the story in a place that matches the story setting).

- Materials and activities related to the text (e.g. feathers for stories about birds, branches, twigs and sticks for stories which take place in woodland settings).

- Suggestions to encourage children to retell the story in their own words (e.g. through mime, plays, puppets, constructions, small-world settings).

- Ask parents to take a photo or film the activity. Replay the film and encourage children to give opinions and feedback.

- Other outdoor activities – for example, children could go for a walk with their parent through a wood to look for evidence of animals found in a woodland storybook.

Idea 10.7 Physical education

PE is probably the one activity that most primary teachers have taught outside at some point. As a consequence, children are more likely to know the routines and systems around undertaking PE activities outside. Revisiting your PE curriculum and further developing outdoor sessions can be a good focus for developing the habit of working outside in other curriculum areas. For example, relay races can be used to collect answers to maths problems laid out at the other side of the playground.

Being outside also offers physical experiences that are hard to gain inside, such as:

- Moving over uneven natural surfaces, which increases coordination and balance.

- Encountering a variety of features found in natural landscapes, which means the experience is always slightly different (e.g. balancing on logs, jumping off tree stumps).

- Learning to cope with the seasons and weather (e.g. how to avoid slipping on ice, keeping hydrated in hot weather).

- Participating in informal physical activity through play at breaktimes and also experiencing higher levels of movement when working outdoors.

- Being involved in learning traditional dances which take place outside.

- Experiencing and developing skills in specific physical activities (e.g. orienteering, hillwalking, water sports, Parkour, cycling, skateboarding).

The cumulative impact of adventurous and physical activities outdoors needs to be considered in terms of its contribution to children's general health and well-being. They are also hooks for those children who may not engage in traditional sporting activities. Contact your local outdoor

education team to develop a challenging progression of adventurous activities and to enable wider access beyond formal learning.

Idea 10.8 Get your class to create outdoor activities

Ask the children to choose a theme or concept that is related to their class project. Then challenge them to work in small groups to develop a plan for creating an outdoor activity to help explain it. The children may need to decide:

■ What is the challenge – what skills, knowledge or understanding will it help others learn?

■ Why do they need to undertake this?

■ What are they going to do and how?

For this to be effective, ensure that the children work outside – this will help them to generate ideas and make connections. In turn, each group's activity can then be undertaken by the whole class, followed by a discussion about what worked well and why it helped the children to understand the particular concept being taught. Remember to set clear timescales for this activity and remind children that often it is the simplest ideas which are most effective.

In my experience, natural environments, such as beaches and forests, naturally lend themselves to thinking creatively about the curriculum. For example, when looking at the concept of levers outside, once children know the basics about levers, they will quickly come up with examples, such as mobiles made from sticks and seesaws created from balancing one log on top of another.

Idea 10.9 Create finishing tasks

It is always helpful to have some finishing activities up your sleeve so that children can be meaningfully engaged whilst their peers complete the main task.

Discuss ideas with children and put together a shared list of activities. Encourage the children to come up with suggestions that require the minimum of preparation and resources that can be found outside. Here are some ideas to kick-start the possibilities:

- Strategy games, e.g. noughts and crosses or Nim (Idea 4.18).
- Outdoor doodles and sketches using pencil and scrap paper (Idea 5.18).
- Pictures created using chalk on asphalt.
- Simple poetry formats (e.g. acrostics based on the local area or things the children can see outside) – put together a bank of ideas.
- Read a book (Idea 10.5).
- Invent a game and play it with someone else who has finished.
- If there are playground markings for games, then play one of these.
- Compile a variety of scavenger hunts linked to ongoing work in different subjects (Ideas 7.10, 7.11 and 7.12).

Idea 10.10 Use digital technology outside

Mobile devices are designed to be used in different places. Make the most of their portability and have them ready to use in outdoor sessions. In principle, these devices are very economical in terms of resources – for example, many have in-built cameras, video and audio recorders, calculators, weather apps, compasses and GPS devices.

As such, digital devices have a lot of potential as tools for record-keeping. For example, there are packages available which allow photos and observations to be directly uploaded to children's individual records. Just make sure such applications reduce rather than create workload.

In my experience, most children are not obsessed with technology but take a pragmatic approach to its use. When outside, children might be interested in using technology but this rarely detracts from the predominant purpose of an activity. Have a basic agreement in place that the device is to be used strictly in line with the purpose of the task.

However, do remember that children like time to explore gadgets – it is an aspect of their playful approach. This could be incorporated either as part of an introduction to using a new tool or as a useful finishing task. Also, it is quite likely that they will be able to advise you on decent apps for different jobs and will be happy to share their expertise!

I have found the best way to get ideas about using specific digital technology in activities outside is to put a call out on different education forums and social media sites.

Linking outdoor and indoor learning

It is important to consider the flow between outdoor and indoor learning. If outdoor sessions work in harmony with indoor activities, and vice versa, this can be helpful in terms of enabling children to make connections and transfer skills into different contexts.

Without this flow, it's a bit like bursting a balloon. The outdoor party is over – now let's get back to work. This is the sort of message which further reinforces the myth that real work can't happen outside.

Idea 10.11 Create a discovery table

A discovery or nature table should invite children to touch, explore, experience and ask questions. Good presentation will encourage children to visit the table, so spend time experimenting and working on this until you get the appearance and layout right – the children could also advise you. Things to consider include:

- Natural items look wrong in plastic containers, so collect alternatives (e.g. log slices to present items on). You can also pick up little baskets from charity shops and ethical trading companies. Glass bottles and ceramic containers are a good option for holding and storing items – they are great for making shakers and rattles too.

- Wooden chopping boards are good surfaces for displaying things or for children to use when using or examining different objects.

- Boxes which can be opened up.

- Presentation stands or shelves.

- Drawers, trays or some form of storage system.

- Keep the background plain or put a mirror behind the display to add interest.

- How many children you want to be able to access the table at the same time.

The following may be useful for close-up observation:

- Digital microscope.

- Magnifying glasses of different strengths.

- Fresnel lenses.

- Rulers for checking the sizes of different objects.

- Tweezers for dissecting items.

- Mirrors for looking under things – dental mirrors can be particularly useful.

- An iPad, or other digital device, for photographic exploration, creating animations or short videos and for identifying mystery objects through Internet research.

The whole point of a discovery table is for it to be a place of investigation. Encourage children to add comments and ask questions. Leave out supplies of materials for this purpose, such as:

- Cream or off-white recycled paper – complements natural materials well.

- Buff luggage tags.

- Large lolly sticks.

- Tracing paper.

- Flattened leaves – write on these using a black marker pen.

- Old CD-ROMs.

Ensure the table changes in line with the seasons, ongoing projects, children's interests and items they have brought in. Possibilities include:

- Growing things (e.g. plant cuttings, bulbs, pips, seeds and stones from fruit and found items such as acorns). Try growing the tops of root vegetables, such as carrots, parsnips and beetroots, by placing them in a shallow dish or saucer of water.

- Creating miniature worlds, tiny landscapes and little gardens (e.g. desert gardens, Zen gardens). Try creating bottle gardens too.

- Making homes for minibeasts. Keep worms, slugs or snails for a day or two before returning them to their homes outside. Set up an aquarium for fish or amphibians, or a formicarium for ants.

- Skulls and bones – make sure they are clean. It is worth asking nature centres and outdoor professionals if they have examples that can be borrowed.

- Collecting dead minibeasts to dissect and examine under a microscope (but don't kill for this purpose – seize the moment when a dead animal is found that is still fresh enough to observe).

- Creating citrus 'boxes' – cut oranges or grapefruits in half, scoop out and use the flesh, then place the rinds onto the bottoms of plastic bottles to dry out.

- Rocks, stones and fossils – invite a geologist or rock enthusiast to come and admire the collection.

- Driftwood, shells and seaweed.

- Twigs of different shapes and colours, and from various species.

Encourage the children to bring in items from home. This could be part of a homework task (e.g. find an interesting leaf).

Idea 10.12 Get arty with found material

Create a natural art store. This is a clever way of extending art resources. Collect together the following types of material in containers for children to use:

- Seeds and seed heads – lavender, coriander and sweet cicely seeds are particularly useful because they smell nice too.

- Cones of different sizes and species – great for making little creatures.

- Washed fleece and gathered wool – this is good for weaving projects

- Clay – show children how to roll it out, use cutters and press natural objects into the clay. Remove for imprints or leave in shells and stones to make mosaics. Bake in the sunshine!

- Leaves – make leaf rubbings, then cover with PVA glue before threading together and hanging up as leaf bunting, or make leaf silhouettes by painting over and around them before removing the leaf to leave the outline. Explore different ways of printing with leaves by doing an Internet search.

- Long grasses and thin twigs for weaving.

- Stones for painting and decorating.

- Small twigs for line work.

- Feathers for texture, printing and painting.

- Flowers for adding colour. Sea glass is great too.

- Scrap cardboard to frame pictures or for showing children how to frame their creations.

Idea 10.13 Teach children to press leaves and weeds

Show children how to press collected leaves and common weeds. It is a method of flattening and drying them so that they retain their colour for longer and can be used decoratively in collages and displays. Leaves will curl up within a few days if they are not pressed flat.

If you are short of funds, then use sheets of toilet paper or kitchen roll. Tear off several sheets and lay them flat on an open page in a large hardback book. Lay the leaves and flowers on the tissue paper. Put further sheets of tissue over the leaves and flowers so they are covered. Close the book. Add lots of other heavy books on top and leave them to press for two weeks. If you have more funds at your disposal then you can buy a flower press.

Having an ongoing supply of dried leaves and flowers can be great for formal and informal art activities, such as making greetings cards and bookmarks – laminate them if you want the materials to remain in place. Make pressing into a job for a couple of children every time leaves or flowers are brought in.

Idea 10.14 Journals

If you enjoy using journals with students, then get children to make ones for outside use – they need to be robust enough to withstand the elements. If you want children to add flowers, leaves and other natural materials to their journals, then cream or black card works well as these colours seem to complement natural colours nicely.

There are many books which give advice about creating and keeping journals and different ways of recording thoughts, feelings, experiences and ideas. For some ideas, do an online search for 'how to journal'. The journals do not have to be entirely literacy-based but could include drawings and collaged images or objects.

Journals can be used to:

- Write up poems that were created outside.

- Collate questions about the outdoor world.

- Assemble sketches and doodles done outside – cut out and stick in the book, then add a detailed border.

- Develop advice notes about different topics or subjects.

- Create collections of similes, metaphors and alliterations inspired by work undertaken outside.

- Stick a pressed leaf or flower in the middle of the page and use to create a unique piece of artwork.

- Make thought clouds – ideas and thoughts that float through your head as you watch clouds pass by.

- Record group or class work. This can be a collaborative approach to reflecting and thinking about an event or an idea which has arisen from an outdoor activity. Use big sheets of card or heavy paper which will allow everyone to contribute to one class journal.

Journals can also work well as a way for children to summarise their thoughts about an outdoor session back in the class. A useful trick is to give out just one piece of card after each session. As the weeks go by, the journal gets built up, sheet by sheet. This means you have not spent money on expensive shop-bought journals and aren't left with lots of blank pages and guilt. Once the term or year has finished, the children can be shown simple binding methods to turn the sheets of card into a handmade book and can explore crafty ways of creating a beautiful cover – do an Internet search for some ideas.

Idea 10.15 Share your outdoor experiences with the world

Collaborative projects between schools within and beyond the UK are great for children to share outdoor experiences. When writing a blog, tweeting or setting up a wiki, it is important to have an audience who will be responsive to the children's efforts. Having several schools that are willing to read and respond to each other's work can make a real difference to levels of interest and enthusiasm.

Idea 10.16 Naturalise your indoor space

How your classroom is laid out, and what is displayed inside, gives children and visitors clear messages about your values. Introducing a more natural indoor environment will suggest that the focus is changing. Swedish outdoor primary schools have a feeling akin to an outdoor centre. There is usually sufficient space to hang up lots of outdoor clothing. Inside, nature predominates too. For example:

- Mobiles made from branches are used for visual displays.
- Natural treasures, such as collections of stones, are displayed on shelves.
- Baskets and wooden bowls are used to display materials and resources.
- House plants green up the indoor space.
- Calm colours are used for walls and as table covers.
- Information is available about the world outside, such as details about local outdoor and community events. There are also books with outdoor themes.
- Natural materials, such as felt and wool, are used for cosy corners.
- Natural resources, such as acorns, are used as counters.
- There are photos and information displays about outdoor activities.

Whilst there is no need to transform your classroom into a lookalike field studies centre, thinking about its ambience will doubtless influence how you and the children view the relationship between indoor and outdoor spaces.

Idea 10.17 The children and nature design principles

In 2008, David Sobel, a place-based educator, wrote a book called *Childhood and Nature: Design Principles for Education*.[1] In it, he proposed that seven play themes or principles emerge when children have safe, free time in nature. These are adventure, fantasy and imagination, animal allies, maps and paths, special places, small worlds, and hunting and gathering.

Sobel suggests these principles are common to children anywhere, irrespective of their country, background, climate or culture. They are not linked to developmental stages within childhood but will manifest themselves in different ways as a child grows older. For example, hiding in a cardboard box could be a pre-school child's special place. In middle childhood, children will build forts and dens, away from the adult eye. During the teenage years, young people might create more permanent structures, such as a shack to hang out in with friends. The themes do not operate in isolation – sometimes children can be playing a game or doing something that covers a multitude of themes.

---

1 Sobel, *Childhood and Nature*.

Sobel advocates using the seven design principles to help plan learning experiences when working with children of all ages. They will enable you to provide appealing child-centred experiences during class time and a valuable bridge between free play and formal learning.

To help you use these principles effectively, look at your current plans for the term ahead. Think about the principles as springboards to planning creative learning experiences in any curriculum area. I've found the principles particularly useful for approaching literacy.

Principle 1: Adventure

This is about constructing adventures, setting personal challenges, taking risks and having opportunities to retell the story afterwards. An adventurous experience provides a springboard into the retelling of an event. It is a context for examining the sequence of events and the concept of a decent plot or storyline.

Principle 2: Fantasy and imagination

This is about living and re-enacting challenges and life experiences rather than simply studying them. It may involve having an imaginary friend, acting out scenarios with play figures or becoming these characters, drawing on role play, or using stories or films to inspire. This type of play can help to develop and understand characters when writing stories.

Principle 3: Animal allies

This is about children's friendships with animals. They will pick them up, hold them close, care for them, become them, wear animal costumes or masks, and welcome opportunities to stumble across and find life. This is an important precursor to understanding biodiversity and developing empathy. Without empathy, it is hard to write from different perspectives or see alternative points of view. It can be an asset when constructing arguments or engaging in formal debates on different subjects.

Principle 4: Maps and paths

This principle includes map making, following paths, way-finding activities, figuring out short cuts, and developing an awareness of place and one's existence in the world. Many children love making trails and treasure hunts. It is a great way of learning about a local area or natural space. It is also teaches them about giving and following directions and the sequencing and ordering of events and instructions. Creating trails and following them provides a context for children to learn about functional writing forms such as writing letters, reading maps, and discovering the variety and uses of environmental print.

Principle 5: Special places

Dens offer children the possibility to hide away. Children like to create homes away from their home as a bridge to the wider world. They can be places to bond with the natural world, allowing children to feel comfortable in the landscape, connected to it and eventually committing stewardship acts. Dens also provide great hideaways where a child can write in peace. Have a look at the ideas in Chapter 5 for literacy activities that can be undertaken within a den-building context.

Principle 6: Small worlds

Many stories are created and acted out in the context of a tiny world. Children become creators and destroyers of their little places. It is also a way of enabling children to have authentic experiences without requiring replication on a huge scale. This can be used for scene-setting in creative writing and also to lead into activities which develop children's understanding of sustainability. As impact can be monitored easily, small worlds can make the abstract more concrete – for example, creating a miniature world and then flooding it with water can help children to understand the damage caused by flooding.

Small worlds can also provide themes such as 'Fairyland'. For example, as part of a themed project, I have created fairy dust trails which lead to a basket and a letter asking children to build the fairies new homes as a big dragon has destroyed their old ones. Could they build dragon-proof houses? The children then design and create their fairy houses. They produce advice and tips for the fairies about the dragon-proofing measures built into each house. The children know when their houses have become occupied by fairies because they would become invisible to the human eye! This was my way of ensuring that the houses could be quietly removed before getting accidentally damaged during lunchtimes and breaktimes.

Principle 7: Hunting and gathering

This involves a range of hunting and gathering games: fishing, capturing animals, collecting treasures, scouting, climbing, throwing activities, capture the flag, kick the can, hide 'n' seek, bushcraft skills and so on. A lot of this is about developing practical skills in a social context. Very often, traditional games can be adapted and applied to different projects or to help learn specific concepts in different curriculum areas. Games can also be modified to help develop key literacy skills, such as spelling, punctuation and grammar. Instructions can be written by children for different hunting and gathering-type activities.

Keeping the Momentum Going checklist

Have you:

- ■ Allocated sufficient time to plan and prepare your outdoor activities?

- ■ Ensured that you have included follow-up work back inside the classroom after each outdoor session?

- ■ Considered displays and activity tables which enable children to continue learning inside from the outdoor experiences?

- ■ Begun to include outdoor homework activities and linking outdoor work to texts?

- ■ Shared your outdoor experiences with others, and vice versa, for mutual continuing support and inspiration?

CHAPTER 11

Nagging Doubts, Fears and Worries

This chapter is about the fears and concerns that teachers have when undertaking learning outdoors. Very often, there are no right answers or approaches that fit all situations. It is a case of having to experiment, adapt and find out what works in your unique circumstances.

Often, practitioners look to experts to solve problems or come up with answers. But think about who knows your class, school grounds and local area best – it is likely to be yourself, other teachers, the children, and the school and wider community. I have found that teachers who make the effort to go outside regularly become attuned to the environment and how children are outside. They become outdoor experts in their own right.

Idea 11.1 I hate being outside

You will be pleased to learn there are plenty of outdoor educators who work outside with children on a daily basis, who don't go rock climbing at weekends but prefer to stay in and watch Saturday night TV after spending a day in town with friends!

And just because someone likes being outside, it doesn't mean they will be a good teacher out there either. That would be like presuming that an individual who likes children will be a natural teacher, or that you will never understand parents if you are not a parent yourself.

Consider why *not* liking being outside might work to your own and your children's advantage. As a result, you will be sensitive to children who are not coping and may be in a good position to provide appropriate support. You may understand a child's disinterest in some aspect of outdoor work, such as studying plants, and thus think of creative ways of approaching these activities.

If you want to really analyse yourself, then think about what you *do* like about being outdoors, even if it's not your first choice of place. For example:

- Lying on a beach
- Having a barbecue
- Watching a sunset
- Gardening
- Playing paintball in a wood
- Walking your dog
- Spending time with your children outside

Focus on these positive situations and use them to help you plan outdoor activities for your class. For instance, if you enjoy walking your dog, then devise a Homemade Dog Show. This is where children find out what happens at a dog show and then create a similar experience for their soft toys or homemade dogs.

Idea 11.2 Should I take my class outside in horrible weather?

As a general rule of thumb, I find working outside to be manageable in most weathers. I keep a sharp eye on the children's well-being and tend to stick to shorter periods of time outdoors if I am at all concerned about weather conditions.

From time to time, I will postpone an activity because of bad weather. Generally, this is when it is very wet and windy. Doing an activity in gale-force conditions under trees is not good practice. Similarly, when a thunderstorm is right overhead and fork lightning is blitzing the playground, stay inside.

Below are some of the factors to consider when making decisions about taking children outside during inclement weather:

- Find out what the children would prefer – ask them if they are up for an outdoor activity or whether it would be better to postpone it, if this is possible.

- Enjoy it – some children have never experienced really wet and windy weather. Let them play out and then use the experience as a springboard for some indoor work.

- Make sure the children have appropriate outdoor clothing and footwear. (See Idea 2.15 for advice about suitable clothing.)

- Stick to activities which involve moving about – do the bits that involve sitting around inside.

- Have an alternative inside activity prepared.

- Go out once the weather improves.

Idea 11.3 Can my class work in the school grounds without an adult being present?

Whether your children can work unsupervised will depend on your school. Every school, class and child is different, so it is hard to make generalised statements as to whether this is suitable for your situation.

You will, of course, be supervising the children remotely. This can be a good way of building trust and developing the children's independence. It is wise to carry out a risk–benefit assessment around remote supervision and put in place routines and strategies to manage any identified risks.

Various approaches can be taken, but the following have worked well for different ages and classes:

■ There is a system in place whereby the teacher knows who is outside at any given moment in time.

■ Children are only allowed to work outside if they can be trusted to do so and in the agreed designated place and time.

■ If there is a problem or difficulty, then the children have to sort it out promptly or else come back inside.

■ There must be a minimum of three children together at any given point. If one child gets hurt, then one can remain with the injured child whilst the third child goes for assistance.

■ The children know what to do if an unexpected person or animal turns up. Likewise if the fire alarm goes off – they should know what to do and where the assembly point is.

■ The head teacher and parents are aware that outdoor activities are taking place and know and understand why you are doing this. If a parent is concerned, then spend time explaining how it will work and the procedures you have put in place to ensure this is as safe as necessary.

If the children are working just outside the classroom, then you can also rearrange the layout inside so that you can look out of the window and see what is happening from where you sit.

Idea 11.4 Do I need to get rid of all the poisonous plants in the school grounds?

The whole concept of a poisonous plant needs careful thought. It's an ambiguous label which can lead to confusion. So much depends on the tolerance of a person or animal to a toxic chemical, the strength and quantity of the chemical (which can be affected by the time of year or maturity of a plant), the level of harm caused by ingestion or use, the numbers of people affected each year and so on. This is why the term 'potentially harmful plant' is used instead.

According to John Robertson, a former warden of the Poison Garden at Alnwick Castle, in North-umberland: '"Harmful" is a very significant word when it comes to poison plants. A plant can be as poisonous as it likes but, if there is nothing about it that encourages you to engage with the poison, it can never be harmful.'[1] There are many potentially harmful plants all over the place. In many gardens you will find a host of plants including foxgloves, nettles and various berry-producing shrubs amidst the daffodils, snowdrops and rose bushes. All these plants pose risks of one sort or another. Whether it's thorns, stinging leaves, fruit that causes stomach ache or simply that the whole plant is poisonous, we have grown up living with these plants around us.

When you look at lists or books about potentially harmful plants, it is a bit like reading a medical dictionary and feeling ill afterwards – you may start seeing danger everywhere! Some plants are harmful if eaten, whilst others can cause adverse skin reactions if handled. No list or book is fully comprehensive, so using these as guides is not necessarily helpful. Also, a tiny minority of people have allergic reactions to 'safe' plants, that is, one which does not contain any constituents that are toxic to humans when ingested or which commonly cause an adverse skin reaction.

Most school grounds will have a few plants on a 'no-no' list, yet schools will probably have very little logged in terms of accidents or first aid required on account of them. Poisoning is a very rare occurrence, and many potentially harmful plants have benefits to wildlife, so a balanced approach is needed. Consider the following factors:

- Get a gardener or another plant expert to help you and your class identify the plants in your grounds. Knowledge is power. The more you learn about plants, the more informed your decisions will be.

- Educate your class about plants. Many children are genuinely interested in knowing which plants are okay to touch and which are not. Children are generally sensible, and will stay away from potentially harmful plants – after all, who really likes playing in nettles!

- Teach children only to eat harvested fruit and vegetables with the permission of an adult. Sometimes schools decide to grow 'help yourself' crops in a particular raised bed or area of the grounds for this purpose.

- Think about the location of plants. For example, thorny plants are useful inhibitors, so planting a thorny hedgerow can reduce unwanted access to the school and function as an excellent wildlife corridor, which allows animals such as hedgehogs to travel safely. However, planting thorny hedge alongside the football pitch is unlikely to be popular as balls will need to be retrieved.

- Follow any local authority advice that exists, especially over the removal of particular plants.

- Follow your first-aid guidelines if you are concerned about a child being poisoned. Always take a plant sample along if seeking medical advice.

---

1 J. Robertson, *Is That Cat Dead? And Other Questions about Poison Plants* (Brighton: Book Guild Publishing, 2010), p. 7.

■ Wear gloves when gardening and wash your hands after being outside.

Idea 11.5 Is it safe to pick mushrooms?

Mushrooms and fungi grow everywhere – without these species, there would be no life on earth. Children are likely to find some when out and about, especially after a spell of wet weather in autumn, so here are some general guidelines (which also apply to wild berries):

■ The real harm is done when mushrooms and fungi are ingested. Picking mushrooms and fungi tends not to cause an adverse reaction, so do not worry unduly if a child comes running up to you with one clutched in their hand. Just ensure that they don't put their fingers in their mouth and they wash their hands thoroughly afterwards.

■ Use mushrooms and fungi as a learning opportunity. There are lots of free resources and activities on the Fungi4Schools[2] and Nature Detectives[3] websites.

■ Take a sustainable and rights-based approach with children (as outlined in Chapter 1). Rather than dwell on the dangers of mushrooms, encourage children to think more broadly, such as remembering that although it is their right to forage for mushrooms and fungi, it is also their responsibility to know what it is they are picking. Your class may need reminding from time to time that if they pick a mushroom, then other people will not get to a chance to see it. Also, other wildlife may be adversely affected because some species eat mushrooms and fungi.

■ Follow your school's first-aid procedures if a child does ingest a mushroom. If the child needs medical attention, remember to take a sample of the mushroom with you.

Idea 11.6 Bird issues

The Royal Society for the Protection of Birds runs a wildlife enquiries line which anyone can call to ask questions about bird problems. The RSPB website also has lots of information and advice about birds[4] or you can phone your local RSPB office.

Here are some common examples of bird issues:

Gulls are a nuisance in our playground

Firstly, take a problem-solving approach. Ask the children why the gulls are there and talk about their adaptability. Next, ask the children what they can do about the gulls. Very often, gulls visit grounds because of leftover food and litter from playtimes. Interestingly, herring gulls, which often

2 See <http://www.fungi4schools.org>

3 See <http://www.naturedetectives.org.uk>

4 See <http://www.rspb.org.uk>

frequent school grounds, are on the UK Red List owing to their recent rapid decline in numbers.[5] Therefore, it is worth thinking about the role of schools in conserving this species.

A bird has made a nest in our school grounds in an unsuitable place

If appropriate, make some signs warning people to avoid the area until the chicks have hatched. If that is not possible, the nest will probably fail due to disturbance – hopefully, the birds may try to nest again elsewhere.

What do we do if we find a bird's egg or baby bird on the ground?

If an egg is on the ground, it will either be broken or will have become too cold to hatch. Tidy it away or leave it for other birds to scavenge. If you find a baby bird, then put it back in the nest immediately, if you can find it. If not, put the chick in a sheltered or protected place nearby, like a tree or shrub, where the parent birds will find it.

Can we touch or take eggs from a nest?

All birds, their nests and eggs are protected by law – it is illegal to disturb, destroy or take eggs from an active nest. Once the chicks have fledged, and the nest is no longer being used, it is possible to investigate the nest.

Are feathers safe to collect outside?

Yes. It is fascinating to collect different feathers, examine them and find out how they work. There are also some fun activities you can do with feathers on my blog.[6] Always remember to wash your hands after collecting feathers.

Do we only feed the birds in winter?

Winter is when birds need our help most because their natural food sources become scarce, but it is okay to feed birds all year round, particularly in late spring to give them a boost when they are rearing their young. Have a look at Idea 8.26 for bird-feeding activities and advice.

Idea 11.7 I hate bugs and bigger animals

Children disliking certain animals, particularly insects, is a big topic but usually fairly seasonal. At different times of the year, depending on the weather, different animals become more prevalent.

Playing games, singing songs and listening to stories about animals can help to develop empathy. Watching, listening and being around animals can also arouse curiosity and interest in finding out more. (For further suggestions see Chapter 8.)

---

5 See <http://www.rspb.org.uk/wildlife/birdguide/status_explained.aspx>
6 See <http://creativestarlearning.co.uk>

What matters most is that you model a care and appreciation of living things – your behaviour will affect how children perceive and act around animals. If you show obvious dislike and distaste, it can negatively impact on children's perceptions, beliefs and understanding of the natural world. Use spoons and bug boxes to allow closer examination of various minibeasts. Take your time and learn to how to gently hold worms, slugs and snails, and allow yourself to get used to the sensation.

Here are some tips and tricks which help make the experience of being around little animals meaningful and interesting. Any shrieking usually subsides and children become much more receptive to looking and carefully handling creatures. Remember to always return animals to where you found them.

Worms – check its attitude

Does your worm have attitude? Gently, put the worm on the palm of a wet hand:

- If it jumps off, it is king of the compost and has an attitude of 10/10.

- If it wriggles around on your hand, your class may rank it as 5/10.

- If it flops about miserably, then its attitude may only be 2/10 or 3/10. Give it worm first aid, which means gently returning it to the soil.

- If it doesn't move, it may be dead. Arrange a funeral for it.

After it's been raining, gulls and other birds tap their feet on grass and other places where worms are hidden to entice them up to the surface. Your class can see if they can have the same success with tap dancing on the grass!

Slugs and snails

Do your slugs and snails respond to different pitches of humming? This can be a great racing tactic, so let the children observe how their gastropods behave when they hum at different pitches. Then hold a snail or slug race.

Placing slugs and snails on Perspex or a transparent tarpaulin and looking at their movement from underneath is great. You can see how they move along on their one big foot.

Follow the silver trails left by slugs and snails and examine the textures they encounter and how this might impact on where they will travel. Do the trails lead anywhere in particular? Are particular surfaces avoided? What does this tell you about the lifestyle and habits of slugs and snails?

Wasps and bees

In late summer, when nectar becomes scarce, bees and wasps search for sweet substances and can become a nuisance. It is worth discussing this with children, particularly if they choose to eat or drink sugary foods. They also seem to be more attracted to white or neutral colours.

Like a fire drill, a wasp drill can be practised prior to any wasp appearing:

- The teacher makes a buzzing sound.

- The children stop, stand absolutely still and keep their mouths shut.

- When the 'wasp' comes near a child, they calmly and slowly walk away.

If a real wasp does appear, taking these steps can reduce the chances of being stung.

Another way of helping children overcome their fears is to discuss them. Short writing activities, such as an advice sheet on 'How to avoid being stung' or 'What to do if a wasp stings you', can be quite effective.

Collecting dead wasps (e.g. from a windowsill) can also be useful, so children can look at them under a microscope. How big is the sting and can it be seen?

Spiders

The world of spiders is an amazing one. Sadly, some spiders do bite when they feel threatened so take care. Use a bug box or plastic cup and teaspoon to gently lift and carry a spider out of harm's way. Here are some other ideas to familiarise children with spiders:

- Stories about Anansi the Spider are well-known in many countries. He is a trickster who takes the shape of a spider. This can be a good start to finding out more about spiders and thinking about the personalities of those in our homes and gardens.

- Hunting for spiders' webs on foggy mornings or after rainfall can be an absorbing activity. Is there a pattern to where the webs are located?

- There are various team challenges that use the concept of a spider's web in a problem-solving capacity. A simple version involves children working in groups. Each group has a ball of brightly coloured wool which is used to create a 3D web. The challenge is to make a web course that other groups have to negotiate without breaking any of the strands of wool as they hop over, under and around it. Afterwards, evaluate the success of each group's web and which courses provided the right amount of challenge – not too easy or too hard.

Dogs

If you are working outside the school grounds, it is quite possible that your class will encounter a dog off its lead. Whilst most dogs are fine, follow the procedures in your school's health and safety policy about the appropriate action to take.

In the event of an aggressive dog invading class activities, the children will need to know what to do. The game 'Who let the dogs out?' teaches children how to respond appropriately. In this game, an adult is the dog inside a circle of standing children. All together, everyone shouts 'Who let the dogs out?', at which point the adult goes up to a child and says 'Woof! Woof! Woof-Woof!' The child must carefully fold their arms and calmly turn away. Then it is the child's turn to be the dog and the activity is repeated.

Idea 11.8 I know nothing about nature

Do not feel that you have to know the names of all the plants and animals in your school grounds or local area. A flexible approach is best in which you discover, search and experience together with the children. Generally, you know when children are interested because they will ask, 'What's that?' Here are some tips:

- Assemble some simple identification books for children to use which focus on common native plants. The Nature Detectives website has lots of free download sheets which are good starting points.[7] These can be laminated for outdoor use.

- Children also enjoy looking at the illustrations in guide books – take these with you when going outside.

- Every now and then, preferably in different seasons, invite a ranger, naturalist or nature enthusiast to accompany the group and capitalise on their skills and knowledge. They can help with identification and are a mine of useful information.

- Use a website, such as iSpot, where you can register to upload photos of any plant, fungi or animal that you do not recognise.[8] Other registered users will help identify the organism.

- Some parents and grandparents may know local names for plants and animals, and can be wonderful sources of inside knowledge about sighting wildlife locally.

- Take a camera and encourage children to photograph the flora and fauna that interests them. This can be used to create a database of local wildlife and plants.

- Often it is the stories and history of our plants and animals that make them interesting and relevant. It's worth learning little snippets of information for this purpose. A quick Internet search can be a good place to start.

- Hold a moment of appreciation. You do not need to know a name but you can appreciate the qualities of a plant or animal. For example, I never fail to be impressed at how quickly grass grows in the summer. It is amazing how it bounces back after being walked upon. And I love the number of games and activities to do in long grass, such as making a grass whistle.

---

7 See <http://www.naturedetectives.org>
8 See <http://ispot.org.uk>

- When a child asks what something is, try to avoid plunging in and being a 'fountain of knowledge' by naming everything. Referring to the names of plants or animals as part of your everyday conversation is a gentle alternative.

- Do not expect or ask children to always try to identify a plant or animal. Follow the child's lead. If they are really interested and want to know more, then go for it. However, it can be off-putting if an adult's response is constantly, 'I don't know, but let's find out.'

Idea 11.9 What about children finding and picking up litter?

Children often find litter quite interesting and in many activities they will choose to pick up a piece as a discussion point. Litter levels can also be an indicator of how a school values its outdoor space. The less litter lying about, the less children are likely to drop litter. There are lots of free resources about running whole-school litter campaigns from the Eco-Schools[9] and Keep Britain Tidy websites.[10]

9 See <http://www.eco-schools.org.uk>
10 See <http://keepbritaintidy.org>

Using litter-picking as a punishment is questionable in terms of the message it sends to children. Instead, it is best to have a couple of spare bags so that any litter that is encountered is picked up – aside from obvious nasties, such as broken glass, drug paraphernalia or litter that requires careful disposal.

If you are going to a place off-site, which might have glass, animal scat or other potentially harmful litter lying around, have a chat with the children before setting off about how to avoid contact and what to do if this happens. With little children, fun can be had making this into a game (e.g. jump the dog poo).

Idea 11.10 Will my class use sticks, stones and ropes sensibly?

I have discovered that sticks, stones and ropes tend to bring out the best in children. They value the responsibility that comes with the use of such resources.

When I introduce the use of sticks to my classes, I begin by showing the children one stick and asking them, 'What do you think we will need to remember when using sticks?' The children's responses always include a wide range of suggestions which can be summed up by three basic rules.

The first is to be sensible when using these materials. The second rule is that, if they pick up an object like a stick, stone or rope, they are responsible for it. Thirdly, the children have to know how to use them and where they should be returned to when they have finished with them. I then ask the children what they think of these rules and request that they abide by them.

If a child is not being sensible with an object, then it is immediately removed from them. It will depend on the activity, and the child, as to when they can use the equipment again. Sometimes, it is returned in just a minute; at other times, it might be left until the next session.

If you want young children to be able to use sticks and stones in their free play, it can take a period of acclimatisation if they are not used to using these resources. One approach is to begin with small twigs and then gradually build up to bigger sticks as the children learn how to use them. Beginning short and small also works well with stones and rope. A similar procedure is then followed to that of introducing sticks.

Over the years, I have developed a risk–benefit assessment about the use of these materials, based upon the procedures outlined above, and which takes account of the specific hazards associated with each resource and how to manage the risks identified. This includes reference to the level of supervision, instruction in use, the quantity of the resource, and how they are stored and made available to the children. This will vary according to the age, ability and character of the children, so I revisit the risk–benefit process for each new group or class of children. It also depends on how well I know them and whether I have additional supervisory staff. I have found this risk–benefit process to be particularly helpful when working with new classes to remind me of what I need to keep an eye on to ensure that the sessions are relaxed, fun and enjoyable.

Nagging Doubts, Fears and Worries checklist

Have you:

- ■ Made a list of those issues which bother you or worry you about working outside with your class?

- ■ Taken each issue in turn and brainstormed ways of managing or alleviating the concerns? Make a plan of action for every eventuality.

- ■ Asked colleagues, outdoor professionals and others for advice about the concerns you have?

- ■ Ensured you have a small way of celebrating your efforts in developing the habit of teaching outside?

- ■ Thought about how you can assist and advise others with similar concerns? After all, experience counts for a lot!

CHAPTER 12

Embedding Outdoor Learning

This chapter is about how you can reflect on your practice. It aims to give you food for thought about how to embed outdoor activities into your teaching so that it becomes just a part of the way you work.

You can use the suggestions alone, with a colleague or as a whole school. This section also includes ideas for eliciting your children's thoughts. After all, they have a right to be consulted on matters that affect them.

Idea 12.1 What is your vision and what do you value about learning outside?

It is always useful to examine our beliefs and values. I would advocate doing something you enjoy outside first. This might be riding a horse, walking the dog, gardening or chilling out in your back-yard with a barbecue and beverage.

Ask yourself the following questions and try to answer honestly. If possible, try to be outside when you are mulling them over. It may be worth discussing your views with a trusted colleague.

- Why do you want to undertake more learning and teaching outside?

- What are you hoping to achieve?

- What will your practice be like?

It is worth asking your class for their thoughts too, particularly after they have completed an outdoor activity. Do the children in your class share your vision or do they have an alternative view? How can you reach a consensus and have a shared purpose and understanding of learning outdoors? For example, one ten-year-old child once commented: 'If we are working outside the school, then surely you can't tell us what to do. We're not in school.'

Idea 12.2 Dream outdoors

Set aside time for dreaming. If you could imagine the perfect outdoor lesson, or school, what would it look like?

- What will you be doing? What will you see and hear happening? How are you feeling?

- What about the children in your class?

- What about the outdoor spaces and places? What will they look like and how will they be used?

- How does it all work?

Dreams like these take time to imagine, so start writing down your ideas in an accessible place so that you can easily add to them. This is an important part of the vision. It's also worth asking other people for their thoughts too. It makes for a good discussion!

The children in your class can also help. Ask them to draw annotated pictures about their thoughts. Help them to build up an ideas box. It can be a useful form of monitoring to get them to undertake this activity at the start and end of a school year, and to compare the pictures they produce.

There are two reasons why this is a good exercise to do. Firstly, it is about creating a vision in a playful way. Secondly, it allows you to add ideas and concepts when they arise. From here, you can start planning for the next steps. For example, if you dream of working in a school in a forest there are several possible ways forward:

- Move to a school in the middle of a wood.

- Find a wood and start the process of adopting it for use by your school.

- Bring the wood to the school – start a programme of tree planting and greening your grounds.

Idea 12.3 Quantitative mapping

Quantitatively reviewing your practice can enable you to identify the amount, time of year and type of activities you have tried.

Look back over the past year and think about what learning you have undertaken outside with your class(es). Map this out in a grid (like the one below) to help you remember what your class did and when. It does not matter if you were at a different school, had a completely different class of children or are a student – this is still a helpful reflective exercise.

A year outdoors

Month	School grounds	Local area (off-site, walking distance)	Requiring transport (day visits or longer elsewhere)
September	Read a story outside to the class Played traditional games as part of a whole-school playground project		
October			
November	Planted trees as part of National Tree Week		
December		Sang carols at local old folk's home	
January		Forest School – six sessions for half the class, swapping over at half term. Organised by deputy head teacher	
February			
March			
April	Put bedding plants into containers at the school entrance		
May	Class undertook three data handling sessions outside linked to bird project	Went bird watching in local woods with RSPB volunteer	
June	Sports day – two practice sessions plus the actual event		Visited RSPB reserve as part of a bird project
July	Visiting storyteller worked outside with classes		
August			

Once you have completed your grid, look at the range of activities and when and where they happened:

■ How many of the activities are self-generated as opposed to being driven by whole-school events or policy?

- What is the balance like across the curriculum areas? What about making the most of informal learning opportunities during lunchtimes, after school and during the holidays?

- What is the spread of activity throughout the year? Is there a balance or more happening at certain times?

- How many activities are led by other people rather than yourself as the class teacher?

- What does this grid tell you about your current use of the outdoors?

Keep hold of this grid – it is a useful benchmark. If you repeat the exercise after twelve months, it will show you how your practice has changed in terms of the quantity, type and spread of outdoor activities.

What now?

If you want to move to a situation where learning happens outside on a frequent and regular basis all year round, then it is up to you! It is highly unlikely that your school will be able to afford more than one or two excursions which involve paying for transport. It is also probable that paying for professionals to visit your school and work with your class will be an exceptional event rather than a regular opportunity. There are various ways in which this can be achieved, such as the outdoor calendar (see Idea 12.4).

Idea 12.4 An outdoor calendar

Looking at learning opportunities outside across a whole year follows on nicely from the quantitative mapping exercise (see Idea 12.3). There are several reasons for taking a monthly calendar approach.

Firstly, gardening advice, religious events and other seasonal events are mapped out in terms of calendar months. You can make the most of each season and the multisensory learning opportunities that go hand in hand with this.

Secondly, it allows for a whole-school approach where classes can join together for some activities, assemblies can be planned around themes, and continuity and progression are assured. Each class can have a grid (see the example below) which can feed into a whole-school calendar. This can be a good way of ensuring progression within a school.

The table on page 190 is an example from my own practice. You will notice that the first row covers the maintenance aspects of managing school grounds or another patch of ground (e.g. an allotment or woodland). Very often, these tasks are done as 'extras' rather than as part of the routine weekly or monthly activities within a class. The trick is to integrate them into the curriculum. Tasks such as pruning are practical skills in their own right. This means that a class naturally takes responsibility for looking after the school grounds and this job is shared more equitably. This tends to be more sustainable than having an Eco Club which does everything or one keen teacher or parent group. It is also more inclusive as every child has the opportunity to learn these skills.

Local and national religious and cultural events, celebrations and seasonal activities feature in the next row. Community events can be included here too. Again, the purpose is to ensure that your planning capitalises on these opportunities. Schools that have successfully embedded outdoor learning are almost always an integral part of their local community. Project Britain has a good starting list of monthly religious, cultural and other events.[1]

It is tempting to just fill the right-hand column with curriculum or subject areas. However, outdoor activities don't naturally lend themselves to being split up in this conventional way – they are too interdisciplinary. Very often, literacy and science integrate naturally with seasonal events. Try to avoid tenuous links though – instead, back-link the fourth column to specific curriculum targets or outcomes. Likewise, if you need to include learning intentions, these are quite easy to insert into the calendar at a place of your choosing.

You should consider taking a broad sweep view of what you are expected to cover within the curriculum at your teaching stage. Highlight the targets or statements which clearly link to outdoor activities – such as fieldwork and town studies in geography or studying local heritage in history. These are your priorities in terms of planning outdoor experiences.

---

1 See <http://projectbritain.com/traditions.html>

Not every outdoor activity has to be totally outdoors. My criterion is that there needs to be an outdoor element at some point, whether that's a local walk, collecting natural materials and so on.

An outdoor calendar – September

Class: ....   Teacher: ....   Month: **September**

	Focus/job	Curriculum activities	Subject/curriculum link
Environmental stewardship and maintenance	Weed raised beds	Examine whole plants and revise names and functions of each part Advice about weeding – tweet for ideas and write a 'top tips' blog post	[In this column add the links from the curriculum you use]
	Collect seeds from dead flowers	Store seeds for planting next year. Also set some aside for the nature art store and discovery table (free access by children)	
Celebrations, events, customs and seasonal activities	Welcome back to school	Outdoor circle time on the first day back, focusing on our aspirations for the year ahead	
	Mnemonic Day (30 September)	Introduce the poem 'Thirty Days hath September'. Children each choose a tricky word they find hard to remember. Outside they use what they see as inspiration to create a mnemonic. Homework follow-up	
Maths	Revise 2D shapes – language and properties	After an introductory activity, use a 2D shape scavenger hunt which focuses on key language and knowledge needed. Discuss where and why particular shapes are used in the environment	

Ensuring outdoor learning activities have a positive impact

When it comes to school-based outdoor learning, there is still work to be done in terms of looking at how we monitor and measure the added value of being outside to any subject or to children's well-being. We also run the risk of killing the joy of outdoor learning if we decide that paper-based evidence is the way to go. It goes against the grain of outdoor learning which serves to question traditional indoor practices.

There is a tendency to talk a lot about the benefits of the outdoors without getting to the nitty-gritty of why it is valuable, exactly how it is making a difference and whether it is sustainable in the long term.

In my experience, there is a subtlety which is missed in many standard self-evaluations and audits. Most do not have a mechanism for considering the interrelationships between people, place and activity, and the potential offered by place in the teaching of all subjects. I also believe that understanding is developed through the practical experience of learning outside and reflecting on those experiences with children, colleagues and other people.

Idea 12.5 Use the Valley Section as an evaluative activity

Sir Patrick Geddes (1854–1932) was a town planner, biologist and educator who strongly advocated a place-based approach to learning throughout his life. He provided us with a framework for considering the role of place when evaluating what outdoor activities we offer children and where they occur. He was fond of visual diagrams, which he called 'thinking machines', as a way of encouraging thoughts and discussions. He wanted them to be used and interpreted flexibly. One

GEOLOGIST   FORESTER   CONSERVATIONIST   FARMER   GARDENER   TOWN PLANNER   FISHER

The Valley Section with basic occupations
Adapted from Kenneth MacLean and Walter Stephen (eds), *Exploration: Get to Know Your Own Place and Work and Folk* (Edinburgh: SPGMT, 2007). By kind permission of the Sir Patrick Geddes Memorial Trust.

of his most famous thinking machines is the Valley Section, which was inspired by the River Tay in Scotland and the Ganges in India. The journey a river makes through its watershed from the mountains to the sea covers a multitude of habitats.

When it comes to evaluating the range of possibilities offered by learning outside, I find the Valley Section particularly helpful, both as a class teacher and when looking at outdoor learning at a whole-school level.

Firstly, the diagram shows the relationship between people, places and activities within our society. Where you live affects the activities you can do there, both as a child and as an adult. Schools can exploit their location to celebrate the uniqueness of that place and its rich cultural and natural heritage. Comparisons can then be made with schools in other parts of the UK or the world.

Next, the range of land forms, habitats and land uses identified provide a useful indicator of the breadth of the outdoor activities available to you. If you have undertaken the quantitative mapping exercise (see Idea 12.3), you will be in a position to assess whether there is an overemphasis on one activity over another. For example, a school with a nearby farm is likely to do excellent work in this area, and rightly so. However, opportunities to visit the seaside and study marine life may be missing. When a school considers the progression of learning experiences offered to children as they move through the school, the Valley Section can provide a useful visual audit tool.

Sir Patrick Geddes was keen for the Valley Section to be used for interdisciplinary learning across a variety of curriculum areas. He advocated taking a subject, such as maths, and brainstorming its relevance to real life. For example, you could look at mountains and various occupations, and consider which mathematical concepts might be useful to both learning about landscape formation and undertaking that occupation in a mountainous area. So, a geologist will need to know how the surface area and volume of materials extracted might impact on the profit margin of the company. In contrast, someone who is part of a mountain rescue team will need to understand compass directions and bearings in order to locate lost hikers. She will need to be able to calculate how long it might take to walk a distance up a hill, which would cover the relationship between speed, distance and time. At a simpler level, this may translate into a young child learning that rocks of a similar size may have very different weights, depending on the minerals that formed them. The application of textbook maths to real-life contexts is a useful indicator of how much a child understands a particular concept.

The Valley Section provides us with an open-ended way of thinking about *how* we teach. It can form the basis for reflecting more deeply about embedding outdoor and place-based approaches that goes beyond a tick-box mentality.

What does your class think?

As well as looking at your own practice, it can be helpful to gauge the thoughts and feelings of your class about learning outside. This can provide insight into what is working and what needs more fine-tuning. We need children to be engaged in moving the school forward – their vitality and perspective can ignite enthusiastic change.

There are many ways of eliciting children's thoughts. It can be useful to consider methods which allow you to easily revisit and review children's perspectives.

Idea 12.6 Create an online survey

Use a free tool, such as Survey Monkey,[2] to set up an online survey. Alternatively, some blogging platforms have formats which can be utilised. This works best with older children who can also be involved in deciding what questions should be asked to elicit the most helpful information. It can be great for comparative purposes and action-based research.

Idea 12.7 Ask children to write down their advice

Ask your class to write to you, as their teacher, about what to remember about learning outdoors and their top tips for a successful lesson.

Idea 12.8 Have a whole-class discussion

What do children remember about their learning experiences outside? This can be an excellent precursor to undertaking more outdoor learning. It is a good opportunity to use a thinking skills approach as advocated by Edward de Bono.[3] Get the children to tell you their thoughts and note down in a table (like the one below) the plus, minus and interesting aspects of learning outside in the school grounds, local area or further afield.

	Plus	Minus	Interesting
School grounds			
Local area			
Further afield			

2 See <http://www.surveymonkey.com>
3 E. de Bono, *De Bono's Thinking Course* (London: BBC Books, 2004), pp. 18–24.

Idea 12.9 Problems and solutions

If your class has had negative experiences of learning outside, then focusing on problems and solutions is one way forward. Ask the children to list their problems, and then divide the class into groups and give each group one of the issues. Their job is to brainstorm solutions to this problem. For example:

Problem: We hate being cold outside.

Possible solutions:

- Remember to bring jacket, hats, gloves and other warm clothes to school.

- Wriggle your toes in your boots when standing still.

- Remind the teacher to give out the instructions inside and not keep us standing around outside for too long.

- Have stone hand warmers available to take outside. (These are smooth, rounded pebbles which can be placed in hot water for several minutes to warm up. They can be quickly dried and placed in pockets for a little extra heat.)

Often, encouraging children to try things as an experiment and report back can help. It is also important to focus on self-responsibility. The children need to learn to cope with working outside and to be accountable for finding ways of managing this, albeit with support and encouragement.

How do you know what quality learning looks like outside?

One of the key concerns many teachers have about learning outside is maintaining the pace and challenge as well as high academic standards.

Once a teacher has embedded outdoor learning, there is no reason to lower standards or to presume that standards will slip if learning takes place outside. Many research studies suggest the opposite happens. Research points to the benefits of spending time outside and the subsequent positive impact on children's well-being and ability to learn.[4] Nevertheless, it is up to every teacher to be able to justify their practice, including any outdoor elements.

The quantitative mapping (Idea 12.3) and outdoor calendar (Idea 12.4) are helpful in terms of monitoring the quantity of outdoor learning, where it happens and the parts of the curriculum

---

4 C. Charles and A. Senauer, *Children's Contact with the Outdoors and Nature: A Focus on Educators and Educational Settings* (Sante Fe, NM: Children and Nature Network, 2012). Available at: <http://www.childrenandnature.org/downloads/C&NNEducationBenefits2012.pdf>

which are being covered. For quality, use common sense and apply the same criteria as you would inside. A good lesson is a good lesson wherever it takes place.

Formative assessment and any models or programmes of teaching and learning can be applied to outdoor activities. Be up for discussions with other colleagues, your line manager and others, and provide specific examples rather than clichéd anecdotes.

As part of your reflections, consider:

- **How effective is what you are doing?**
  Consider improvements over several months. Very often things take time to bed down. For example, a Year 1 class might initially take ten minutes to get ready to go outside. After a term, they may be ready within three minutes. Also consider their ability to work outside. With one special educational needs class, it took me a year to see the difference in the children's ability to cope with being outside in all weathers.

- **How are the children in your class benefitting?**
  Which children seem to thrive when working outside? For example, a shy child might become more talkative outside, or a child who lacks concentration indoors may demonstrate much better on-task focus outside. Their achievement or concerns can be added to each child's record or profile.

- **What's working well and how do you know?**
  What learning seems to happen more easily outside? Are some concepts being more quickly acquired? Are children learning more about the nature in their school grounds?

- **Am I choosing the best context and place for learning?**
  Which children work better back in class if an outdoor activity has happened beforehand?

If you are unsure as to what good practice looks like outside, or you think further work is needed, here are some options:

Idea 12.10 Attend a professional development course

Bear in mind that one-off days or twilights can be less effective than courses which create and support collaborative professional learning environments, such as opportunities to reflect and share plans and progress.

Idea 12.11 Undertake a small-scale action research project

Use an aspect of outdoor learning as a focus for an action research project. This can often be undertaken as part of a master's degree or postgraduate diploma.

Idea 12.12 Work alongside a colleague or an outdoor learning professional

There are many people who work with children in different professional capacities (e.g. Forest School practitioner, play ranger, outdoor education instructor). Ask for their advice and ideas and set up a series of outdoor activities on the basis of their observations and your discussions. Some local authorities have work placement or job shadowing opportunities.

Idea 12.13 Ask an outdoor professional or experienced colleague to mentor you

Being mentored by an outdoor professional or colleague may involve brainstorming ideas together for lessons, observing each other at work and giving feedback. Undertaking shared outdoor lessons with two classes can work well, especially if time is made afterwards for shared reflection and acting upon those insights in order to improve practice.

Idea 12.14 Get collaborating online

There is a large network of outdoor professionals and teachers on different social media platforms who provide lots of support and advice. This can really help in terms of challenging your own assumptions. I think we all need to be challenged about what we think, say and do in order for our understanding to grow.

Idea 12.15 Do your own thing

Read up about different aspects of learning outdoors and get writing about your own experiences. Build up collections of advice and snippets using an online bookmarking facility. All these activities can help to build a better understanding of what is involved.

Idea 12.16 Visit a school that has an outdoor philosophy

There is a growing number of schools across the UK and other countries which have exemplary practice when it comes to embedding aspects of learning outside. You may have to ask very nicely and a donation to the school fund is often appreciated. It is worth seeking advice as to which school would be most suitable.

For me, the biggest impact came from visiting an outdoor primary school in Sweden. The outdoor element came across as a normal, everyday practice, which was just another facet of their daily life. Steiner Waldorf schools often have beautiful grounds and an ethos of using the outdoors in day-to-day teaching.

The most well-documented UK school with a strong outdoor ethos is the Coombes Church of England Primary School, in Berkshire. The Coombes School demonstrates a focused and creative approach to ensuring that the curriculum is tailored to meet the needs of children through their use of the outdoors. Two books have been written about their work: *The Coombes Approach* by Sue Rowe and Sue Humphries, and *The Creative School* by Bob Jeffrey and Peter Woods.[5]

With any visit to another school, it works best if you think deeply about why you want to go and how you can use the experience constructively. For example, consider how it could help you to achieve your aims for embedding outdoor learning. It also helps if you reflect with other people or perhaps share what you have observed and learned from the visit.

Embedding Outdoor Learning checklist

Have you:

- ■ Audited where you are at now?

- ■ Reflected upon the issues you are facing and put together strategies for addressing them?

- ■ Put together a plan to embed outdoor activities through the year? Aim for at least one outdoor session per week to begin with, if you are working beyond the Early Level/ Foundation Stage, and build up from there.

- ■ Discussed outdoor learning with your children and gauged their thoughts?

- ■ Undertaken some quality checks to ensure your outdoor work is up to scratch?

---

5 See S. Rowe, and S. Humphries, *The Coombes Approach: Learning through an Experiential and Outdoor Curriculum* (London: Continuum, 2012); and B. Jeffrey and P. Woods, *The Creative School: A Framework for Success, Quality and Effectiveness* (London: Routledge, 2003).

Towards a Whole-School Approach

This book has been written for individual teachers with an emphasis on simple, doable activities for a class of thirty children, rather than a whole-school approach to embedding outdoor learning. However, when staff, children and the wider community begin to think deeply about the purpose of education and what experiences matter to children, then learning outside can be put into an even bigger and more meaningful context. Time is needed to make substantial changes and major shifts in teaching. Real things take up real time – think of the joy of walking through an established, well-maintained garden.

A useful starting place for working towards a whole-school approach is Education Scotland's *Building your Curriculum: Outside and In*.[1] It highlights some of the bigger ideas and practical issues which need to be considered. The Council for Learning Outside the Classroom has a schools' accreditation scheme for outdoor learning which may appeal to some schools.[2]

If you are asked to lead on whole-school development, there are several things to bear in mind:

- When schools embed learning outside it is the result of a sustained year-on-year approach, so ensure outdoor learning is not a one-off action on a school improvement plan.

- Whilst you may wish to have outdoor learning as a key action on a school improvement plan, ultimately it should be a part of most other improvement initiatives going on in the school.

- Everyone in the school can play a part. It should not be left to one or two keen individuals or an 'outdoor learning' teacher. Professional learning and development will be needed.

---

1 Education Scotland, *Building Your Curriculum: Outside and In* (2011). Available at: <http://www.educationscotland.gov.uk/images/building_your_curriculum_outside_in_tcm4-656470.pdf>

2 See <http://www.lotc.org.uk/lotc-accreditations/lotc-mark>

- Consider what the purpose is of learning outdoors and the benefits to all children. Establish clear curriculum links and progression of opportunities. It is important that the progression that happens takes account of the developmental needs of the children at different ages.

- Think about how the local community, partner organisations and parents will be engaged in the process – potentially, these sectors are very big allies.

- As with other aspects of school life, financial input makes a positive difference but is not the be-all and end-all. Mindset matters more than anything else.

Whilst the curriculum is one way to embed outdoor activities, there are other ways of implementing lasting change, such as:

- Play and playtimes – remember this is about changing the culture and attitudes towards play, not about buying expensive playground equipment.

- School grounds improvements – this may be to naturalise your school grounds for play, increase the biodiversity value or for another reason. It is best to use a participative approach, as advocated by Learning through Landscapes, the UK school grounds charity.

- Residential opportunities – these need to be well thought through to ensure they do not become a school-time holiday. Also, create a progression of experiences from Early Years through to older children.

- Adopting a local patch of greenspace – this is about getting to know a space off-site really well and caring for it. A good example might be working in partnership with a community wood.

- Gardening, allotment and orchard projects – these can be very holistic, with schools growing food for school lunches and to sell at market stalls.

- Animals and farming – a farm school offers another very holistic approach.

- Forest School or similar model.

- Adventurous activities – this includes consideration of progression through the school and a variety of adventurous opportunities.

The end of the beginning

This may be the end of the book, yet it really is only the beginning of a different way of approaching learning and teaching. Being outside can be a normal part of any learning experience at any time of the year.

Dirty Teaching is complemented by hundreds of blog posts on my Creative STAR website: www.creativestarlearning.co.uk. The 'I'm a teacher, get me OUTSIDE here!' blog began back in 2008. It's my way of sharing my enthusiasm for learning outdoors with the world. Please stop by, say hello and enjoy browsing many more ideas for teaching, learning and playing in all weathers, all year round, outside.

For me, teaching is more than making a difference. It's about our legacy for future generations. Through teaching children we touch the future. By teaching outside, we make it real.

Cross Reference of Ideas to Subject Areas

Reflective development exercises for teachers

Idea

i Have a cuppa
ii Your life in places
iii Look for SUCCES in your lessons
1.1 Know your rights
1.2 Build a tower
12.1 What is your vision and what do you value about learning outside?
12.2 Dream outdoors
12.3 Quantitative mapping
12.4 An outdoor calendar
12.5 Use the Valley Section as an evaluative activity
12.6 Create an online survey
12.7 Ask children to write down their advice
12.8 Have a whole-class discussion
12.9 Problems and solutions
12.10 Attend a professional development course
12.11 Undertake a small-scale action research project
12.12 Work alongside a colleague or an outdoor learning professional
12.13 Ask an outdoor professional or experienced colleague to mentor you
12.14 Get collaborating online
12.15 Do your own thing
12.16 Visit a school that has an outdoor philosophy

Preparatory activities

Idea

2.1 Dress comfortably
2.2 Eat and drink plenty
2.3 Make a plan and share the love
2.4 Play to your strengths and those of your children
2.5 Keep it simple
2.6 Expect the worst but hope for the best
2.7 Activities involving remote supervision
2.8 Finding out how you get outside
2.9 Walking the school boundary
2.10 Explore your local area
2.11 Create a risk–benefit assessment for the use of your outdoor space during class time
2.12 Involve children in the risk–benefit assessment process
2.13 Take a positive approach to risk

Issues

Idea

2.14 Put together a basic set of resources
2.15 Ensure your children have suitable clothing and footwear
2.16 The children who don't want to go outside
2.17 Reduce the possibility of parental complaints
2.18 Inform and reassure your head teacher

2.19 How much time should I be spending on learning outdoors?
2.20 How long should each outdoor session last?
2.21 There isn't enough time for outdoor learning
2.22 The 'challenging' class of children
11.1 I hate being outside
11.2 Should I take my class outside in horrible weather?
11.3 Can my class work in the school grounds without an adult being present?
11.4 Do I need to get rid of all the poisonous plants in the school grounds?
11.5 Is it safe to pick mushrooms?
11.6 Bird issues
11.7 I hate bugs and bigger animals
11.8 I know nothing about nature
11.9 What about children finding and picking up litter?
11.10 Will my class use sticks, stones and ropes sensibly?

Practical suggestions

Idea

10.1 Why indoors?
10.2 Think about the totality of the learning experience
10.3 Spend time developing year-on-year activities
10.4 Use stories as springboards to outdoor activities

10.5 Have books and other texts readily available for reading outside
10.6 Create outdoor book bags
10.7 Physical education
10.8 Get your class to create outdoor activities
10.9 Create finishing tasks
10.10 Use digital technology outside
10.11 Create a discovery table
10.12 Get arty with found material
10.13 Teach children to press leaves and weeds
10.14 Journals
10.15 Share your outdoor experiences with the world
10.16 Naturalise your indoor space
10.17 The children and nature design principles

Computing
Idea

6.12 Use an augmented reality app
6.13 Create a mission
7.5 Geocaching
7.6 Digital trails
7.19 Digital versus paper maps
10.10 Use digital technology outside
10.15 Share your outdoor experiences with the world

English
Idea

3.19 Ask a question
3.20 Twenty questions
3.26 The biography of an object

3.27 Symbols and map making
3.28 The rhythm of words
4.8 Sounds of silence
4.14 Leonardo da Vinci's curiosity challenge
4.15 Think laterally
4.19 Scenes of death and decay
4.25 A sensory review
5 1 How to build the perfect den
5.2 Create real estate
5.3 Investigate the science of den building
5.5 Den building homework
5.7 Old tent day
6.2 Give children time to reflect upon an adventurous experience
6.3 Retell events in an adventurous way
6.5 Create mini writing kits for mini adventures
9.6 Nooks and crannies
9.7 Cracks
10.4 Use stories as springboards to outdoor activities
10.5 Have books and other texts readily available for reading outside
10.6 Create outdoor book bags
10.14 Journals
10.15 Share your outdoor experiences with the world
10.17 The children and nature design principles

Maths
Idea

3.5 Time the class making a perfect gathering circle
3.21 Leaf line-up
3.22 Getting it sorted
3.23 There's angles everywhere

4.9 Sound maps
4.18 Nim
4.23 Line reviews
4.24 Human scattergraphs
5.8 3D shape structures
7.12 Mathematical scavenger hunts
9.9 Windows and doors
9.16 Make the space a fan-ta-stick place to learn

Science
Idea

3.24 The same and different game
4.13 The exact spot
4.14 Leonardo da Vinci's curiosity challenge
4.17 Science I-spy
4.19 Scenes of death and decay
5.3 Investigate the science of den building
5.12 Every breath you take
8.1 Owl ears and listening
8.2 Owl eyes
8.3 Bring birds to you
8.4 Build a nest
8.5 Walk like an animal
8.6 Hold an animal parade
8.7 Be inconspicuous
8.8 Still and silent
8.9 Colour sticks and camouflage
8.10 Adopt an animal
8.11 Step forward with wildlife
8.12 Find and collect frogspawn
8.13 Hatch chickens
8.14 Create minibeast homes
8.15 Put up bird nesting boxes
8.16 Raise trout or salmon
8.17 Consider death
8.18 Time-lapse videos of decay or change
8.19 Gather seeds and grow them

Physical Education

Idea

3.8 Circle the circle
3.9 Follow my leader
3.10 Circle slap
3.11 Fox and squirrels
3.12 Everybody up
3.13 Team challenges and games
3.17 Moving about games
6.8 Make your school grounds
   more physically adventurous
6.11 Link adventurous activities
   to other subjects
7.3 Physical fitness trails
10.7 Physical education

PSHE

Idea

3.1 Make lining up a challenge
3.2 Ambulatory activities
3.3 Create a gathering place
3.4 Establish a gathering call and
   signal
3.5 Time the class making a
   perfect gathering circle
3.6 Sticky circles
3.7 Circle pass
3.8 Circle the circle
3.9 Follow my leader
3.10 Circle slap
3.11 Fox and squirrels
3.12 Everybody up
3.13 Team challenges and games
3.14 Run and touch
3.15 Stone hunt
3.16 Stone angels
3.17 Moving about games
4.1 Sardines
4.2 Sound 'n' seek
4.3 Far apart
4.4 Solitude mapping

4.5 A reflective walk
4.6 Stone meditation
4.7 Finding your special place
4.12 Watch the leaves wave
4.20 Metasaga
4.21 Clay ball collections
4.22 Talking sticks
4.23 Line reviews
4.24 Human scattergraphs
4.25 A sensory review
4.26 Rope review
5.10 A global dimension to den
   building
5.11 Sing songs in different places
6.2 Give children time to reflect
   on an adventurous experience
6.10 Gently stretch children out
   of their comfort zone
8.21 How important is nature?

Drama

Idea

3.9 Follow my leader
3.16 Stone angels
6.3 Retell events in an
   adventurous way
6.4 Undertake drama activities
6.7 Use props to make quick
   changes to an area outside
8.5 Walk like an animal
8.6 Hold an animal parade
8.7 Be inconspicuous
8.8 Still and silent
9.17 Create an outdoor dressing-
   up box

Citizenship

Idea

5.10 A global dimension to den
   building
8.25 Undertake a John Muir
   Award
9.12 Apply grey matter to grey
   matter
9.18 Start developing the school
   grounds
9.19 Get gardening
9.20 Guerrilla gardening
9.21 Leave a positive legacy
   through art
9.22 Adopt your local greenspace

Bibliography

Ball, D., Gill, T. and Spiegal, B. (2013). *Managing Risk in Play Provision: Implementation Guide*. London: National Children's Bureau. Available at: <http://www.playengland.org.uk/media/172644/managing-risk-in-play-provision.pdf>

Beames, S., Nicol, R. and Higgins, P. (2011). *Learning Outside the Classroom: Theory and Guidelines for Practice*. New York: Routledge.

Buzan, T. (2008). *Mind Maps for Kids* (Study Skills). London: Harper Thorsons.

Charles, C. and Senauer, A. (2012). *Children's Contact with the Outdoors and Nature: A Focus on Educators and Educational Settings*. Sante Fe, NM: Children and Nature Network. Available at: <http://www.childrenandnature.org/downloads/C&NNEducationBenefits2012.pdf>

de Bono, E. (2004). *De Bono's Thinking Course*. London: BBC Books.

Education Scotland (2011). *Building Your Curriculum: Outside and In*. Available at: <http://www.educationscotland.gov.uk/images/building_your_curriculum_outside_in_tcm4-656470.pdf>

Education Scotland (2011). *Outdoor Learning: Practical Guidance, Ideas and Support for Teachers and Practitioners in Scotland*. Available at: <http://www.educationscotland.gov.uk/Images/OutdoorLearningSupport_tcm4-675958.pdf> (accessed 20 December 2012).

Fletcher, A. and Kunst, K. (2006). *Guide to Cooperative Games for Social Change*. Olympia, WA: CommonAction. Available at: <http://www.commonaction.org/gamesguide.pdf>

Geography Collective (2010). *Mission: Explore*. London: Can of Worms Kids Press.

Gill, T. (2010). *Nothing Ventured: Balancing Benefits and Risks in the Outdoors*. Nottingham: English Outdoor Council. Available at: <http://www.englishoutdoorcouncil.org/wp-content/uploads/Nothing-Ventured.pdf>

Gleave, J. and Cole-Hamilton I. (2012). *A World without Play: A Literature Review* (London: Play England). Available at: <http://www.playengland.org.uk/media/371031/a-world-without-play-literature-review-2012.pdf>

Godkin, C. (2007). Wolf Island (Markham, ON: Fitzhenry & Whiteside).

Greenaway, R. (n.d.). *Turn-Taking When Reviewing in a Group*. Available at: <http://reviewing.co.uk/articles/turntaking.htm>

Health and Safety Executive (n.d.). *Children's Play and Leisure: Promoting a Balanced Approach*. Available at: <http://www.hse.gov.uk/entertainment/childs-play-statement.htm>

Heath, C. and Heath, D. (2007). *Made to Stick: Why Some Ideas Take Hold and Others Come Unstuck*. London: Random House.

Higgins, P. and Nicol, R. (2011). Professor Sir Patrick Geddes: 'Vivendo Discimus' – By Living We Learn. In C. Knapp and T. Smith (eds), *Sourcebook for Experiential Education: Key Thinkers and their Contributions*. New York: Routledge, pp. 32–40.

Jeffrey, B. and Woods, P. (2003). *The Creative School: A Framework for Success, Quality and Effectiveness*. London: Routledge.

Joyce, R. (2012). *Outdoor Learning Past and Present*. Maidenhead: Open University Press.

Learning through Landscapes (n.d.). *The Good School Playground Guide: Developing School Playgrounds to Support the Curriculum and Nurture Happy, Healthy Children*. Available at: <http://www.ltl.org.uk/pdf/The-Good-School-Playground-Guide1382978938.pdf>

Lester, S., Jones, O. and Russell, W. (2011). *Supporting School Improvement through Play: An Evaluation of South Gloucestershire's Outdoor Play and Learning Programme*. London: National Children's Bureau. Available at: <http://www.playengland.org.uk/media/340836/supporting-school-improvement-through-play.pdf>

MacLean, K. and Stephen, W. (eds) (2007). *Exploration: Get to Know Your Own Place and Work and Folk*. Edinburgh: Sir Patrick Geddes Memorial Trust.

Nicol, R., Higgins, P., Ross, H. and Mannion, G. (2007) *Outdoor Education in Scotland: A Summary of Recent Research*. Perth and Glasgow: Scottish Natural Heritage. Available at: <www.snh.org.uk/pdfs/publications/education/ocreportwithendnotes.pdf>

North Lanarkshire Council (n.d.). *This Place is Like a Building Site! A Report on the Introduction of Loose Materials to Three Primary Schools in North Lanarkshire*. Available at: <http://www.playlink.org/pubs/This_place_is_like_a_building_site.pdf>

Robertson, J. (2008). *I Ur och Skur, 'Rain or Shine': Swedish Forest Schools*. Available at: <http://creativestarlearning.co.uk/wp-content/uploads/2013/06/Rain-or-shine-Swedish-Forest-Schools.pdf>

Robertson, J. (2010). *Is That Cat Dead? And Other Questions about Poison Plants*. Brighton: Book Guild Publishing.

Rowe, S. and Humphries, S. (2012). *The Coombes Approach: Learning through an Experiential and Outdoor Curriculum*. London: Continuum.

Santer, J. and Griffiths, C., with Goodall D. (2007). *Free Play in Early Childhood: A Literature Review*. London: Play England and the National Children's Bureau. Available at: <http://www.playengland.org.uk/media/120426/free-play-in-early-childhood.pdf>

Selhub, E. and Logan, A. (2012). *Your Brain on Nature: The Science of Nature's Influence on Your Health, Happiness and Vitality*. Toronto: HarperCollins.

Sobel, D. (2008). *Childhood and Nature: Design Principles for Education*. Portland, OR: Stenhouse Publishers.

Titman, W. (1993). *Special Places; Special People: The Hidden Curriculum of School Grounds*. Winchester: World Wide Fund for Nature/Learning through Landscapes.

Unicef (n.d.). Fact Sheet: A Summary of the Rights under the Convention on the Rights of the Child. Available at: <http://www.unicef.org/crc/files/Rights_overview.pdf>

Wells, N. M. and Lekies, K. S. (2006). Nature and the Life Course: Pathways from Childhood Nature Experiences to Adult Environmentalism, *Children, Youth and Environments* 16(1): 1–24.

Index

G

H

I

Messy Maths
A Playful, Outdoor Approach for Early Years
ISBN: 978-178135266-3

Following on from the success of *Dirty Teaching*, *Messy Maths* shows you how to reimagine the outdoors through a mathematical lens – providing a treasure trove of suggestions that will empower you to blend outdoor learning into your day-to-day practice. It is not a 'how to' guide, but rather an easy-to-use reference book replete with ready-to-use games and open-ended ideas designed to help children become confident and skilled in thinking about, using and exploring abstract mathematical concepts as they play outside. Many of these ideas and activities are also beautifully illustrated in full-colour photographs throughout the book, making it even easier to jump straight into outstanding outdoor learning opportunities.

Topics covered include: general advice; exploring numbers; number functions and fractions; money; measurement; time; pattern; shape and symmetry; position, direction and movement; data handling; routines; and the mathematical garden. Each chapter features a section on topic-specific vocabulary and expressions to help you integrate this terminology into each area of study, whilst suggestions for embedding maths into routines are also provided to assist in the development of creative, progressive and flexible approaches to everyday situations.